by

Kelly L. Moran

First published in March, 2000 by:

THAXTED COTTAGE

PUBLISHERS

121 Driscoll Way
Gaithersburg, Maryland 20878-5210
(301) 670 0978

Text Copyright 1999 © by Kelly L. Moran
Layout Design Copyright 1999 © by TMD/Dave Stonehouse
Editor: Sue Brown
Photographs Copyright 1999 © - Royal Doulton and Kelly Moran

Photography of Shelley Teacups by High Impact Photography, USA
Photography of Shelley Pattern Books by Northern Counties
Photography, UK

ISBN 0 - 9676925-0-4

Printed and bound in the United States
This book was printed on genuine WESTVACO 100 # Sterling
Ultra Satin paper
First Edition

From the Author

I am a collector of Shelley china. I love it - can't get enough of it. My house reflects my passion for Shelley, fireplace mantels are jammed full, china cupboards are overstuffed, wall cabinets flowing over and now teacups are sitting on top of every flat surface left in the house! In fact, it is difficult to find space to eat dinner as the tables have long since been conquered by my Shelley obsession.

Not only do I have a passion for Shelley, but I adore the multi-coloured all over floral patterns known as chintz. I only have a few pieces of Shelley chintz, but I am eager to see my collection grow. In November of 1998, I had the rare opportunity to see the original Shelley Pattern Books at the archives department of Royal Doulton. The Shelley UK Club had arranged for a one day viewing of these precious records. What I found filled me with excitement. There are many more chintz patterns in those books then anyone had previously imagined. That's when I decided it would be helpful if collectors could see all the different chintz patterns that were produced!

Most of the pieces shown in the following pages of this book were generously donated to me by fellow Shelley collectors. This book would not exist without their willingness to have their treasures photographed. These collectors, many who live in Australia, Canada, South Africa, and the UK, have gone to incredible lengths to help. Thank you to everyone who supplied an example of Shelley chintz. Oh, the temptation to NOT send your pieces back to you!

The purpose of this book is principally to show collectors the chintz that Shelley produced. It is not intended as a price guide, although I have included a teapot rating scale. These ratings reflect my experiences, and illustrate which chintz patterns are more desirable than others. Every effort was made to get complete and accurate information. Experts in both the Shelley UK Club and the National Shelley China Club were frequently consulted. Your help in providing new information and corrections to _Shelley Chintz_ would be greatly appreciated for use in future editions. I look forward to hearing from you about any new chintz discoveries.

I would also like to mention Mr. Raymond Reynolds of the UK. Mr. Reynolds was the last Manager of Decoration at Shelley Pottery. He worked for the company from 1949 until 1966. I have been very fortunate to have Mr. Reynolds as a source of information. He worked with me while I was in Stoke-on-Trent England deciphering the pattern books, instructing me on the complex processes involved with production, as well as sharing stories & recollections from his days at Shelley. He continued to help with the book for many, many months afterwards. I frequently refer to "Ray" throughout the book - my friend and mentor.

Hope you enjoy the book!

Compare

This is a sample of a ceramic transfer litho sheet in the Maytime Chintz pattern. What is interesting to note about the sheet is the dull, muted colours, especially how the reds, the pinks and dark burgundy tones are all very pale. Once the litho was applied to the cup or plate and fired, then the 'true' colours would appear - just as bright and bold as we see them today!

The lithographer would take a cup, cover it with size (a sticky paste) and then lay the Maytime litho face down on the cup. In areas where the cup became smaller the lithographer would make tiny little creases in the litho paper making certain the entire litho sheet made contact with the cup. Then the lithographer would rub the litho down with a semi-dry sponge. Finally the paper was washed away and the cup fired at approximately 800 degrees celsius for about 6 hours.

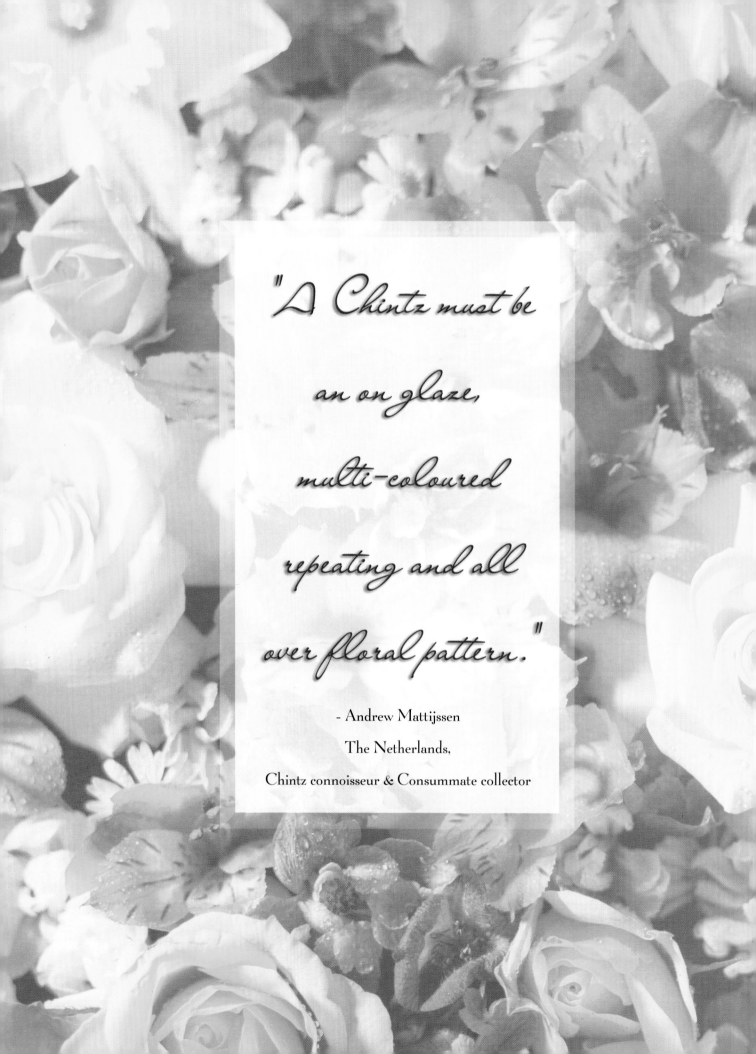

"A Chintz must be

an on glaze,

multi-coloured

repeating and all

over floral pattern."

- Andrew Mattijssen

The Netherlands,

Chintz connoisseur & Consummate collector

Introduction
What Is Chintz, Anyway??

What is Chintz Anyway?

It's been called: Cit, Chit, Cheetes, Schite, Chites, Chint & Chints. It's been sought after, collected, forbidden and outlawed.

We know it today to be a high quality, closely woven polished cotton or linen fabric with a floral design usually showing roses and other varieties of flowers in many different colours. Chintz is a highly durable, hard wearing fabric that is used extensively in England and the United States. The flowers that make up the designs are dense & widespread covering the majority of the surface area, leaving little of the background colour to show through. The word Chintz is Hindi, derived from the Sanskrit **chitra** which means "many - coloured" or "speckled". Chintz has its origins in the textile world, but to truly understand chintz, we must travel to India.

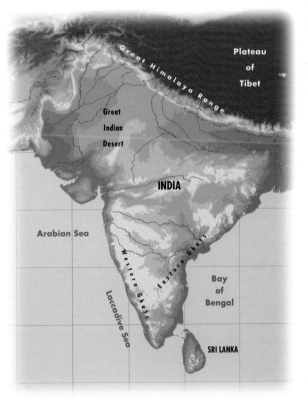

From 1600 to 1800, India was the greatest exporter of textiles the world had ever known. The Indians were the very first to master the skills of painting & printing patterns on to cotton and linen using dyes and pigments with mordants to stop the colours from fading. No one else knew how to do this! Whole villages were employed in producing chintz.

Around 1600, Portuguese and Dutch traders were bringing examples of Indian chintz into Europe.

These early cotton chintz fabrics were extremely expensive and rare with only the wealthy collectors able to afford them. Unlike the fabrics of Europe, which tried to imitate the more expensive woven fabrics of the time, India was producing patterns based on close observation of flora and fauna.

In 1600, the English East India Company was formed by a group of London merchants. Just a year later its first ship sailed east. By the mid 17th century, chintz had become all the rage! Everyone wanted it. The English East India Company imported so much chintz, that everyone in Europe came to know what a chintz was. "By 1680 more than a million pieces of chintz were being imported into England per year, and a similar quantity was going to France and Holland." [1] Daniel Defoe wrote that Queen Mary had a bed hung with chintz "About 1690 at Windsor Castle the late Queen Mary set up a rich Atlas (satin) and Chintz Bed . . . the Chintz being of Masulipatam on the coast of Coromandel, the finest that was ever seen before that time in England."

1 "Chintz and Cotton India's Textile Gift to the World" by Joyce Burnard 1994 Kangaroo Press Pty Ltd. page 16

Let's examine the word "Chintz" more closely. When we peer into the trade records of the English East India Company, we see many variations of the spelling of the word we know as Chintz:

Below are 4 samples taken from the East India Company's records:

1630 - Peter Mundy wrote: "In this place (Sironj) are made great quantities of excellent pintadoes or chints, much nominated and esteemed throughout India."

1652 - Tavernier writes: " . . . embarking on a vessel . . . laden with muslins and chites or coloured calicoes, the flowered decorations of which is all done by hand, which makes them more beautiful and more expensive than when printed."

1665 - Mr. Bernier gives us: " The superior colours of the Maslipatam chittes or cloths, printed by hand . . . are also ascribed to the water peculiar to that town."

1669 - 1679 Bowery writes: "Metchlipatam Affordeth many very good and fine Commodities . . . divers sorts of Chint curiously flowered, which doth much represent flowered Sattin, of Curious, Lively Colours . . . "

With imported chintz becoming so popular with Europeans during the late 1600's, manufacturers of silk & wool in France and England became very concerned. They didn't like this foreign competition and they couldn't produce a similar chintz product! The French were the first to rebel against chintz. In 1686, they declared a ban on all chintz imports.   In England there were " . . . riots in the streets when chintz gowns were torn off the backs of their wearers and the fragments waved triumphantly as banners in processions of protest." Protesters urged Parliament to ban chintz. After several attempts by Parliament to ban the imported Indian chintz, in 1720 they were finally successful. The law forbid:

"the Use and Wearing in Apparel of imported chintz, and also its use or Wear in or about any Bed, Chair, Cushion, or other Household furniture." [2]

Even though chintz was outlawed, there were loopholes in the legislation. It was permissible to import chintz if the final destination was elsewhere in Europe. Many merchants would claim to be re-exporting chintz when in fact they simply sent the ships around the coast to Kent or East Anglia. The chintz would then be sold to the English. In France, where chintz was also banned, the Court of Versailles was outside the law. Fashionable young courtesans went right on wearing their beloved chintz! Chintz was so much en vogue at the time of the ban that bold French women would wear it despite the potential for severe punishment or risk of possible death.

The Dutch never had a ban on the Indian chintz, and throughout the 18th Century, they continued to import it. One traditional Dutch dress very much in demand at the time was called the Wentke - a mourning gown patterned with stylized flowers on a white background. The colours of the flowers went through various stages from near black indigo, to light blue and so on to various bright colours. Dutch chintz fabric was always more boldly patterned and more brilliantly coloured than the English or French chintz.

During the chintz craze that gripped France and England, the textile factories could still not figure out how India was producing it. Leave it to the French! A Naval officer, M. de Beaulieu who was stationed in Pondicherry, India in 1734, was the first to provide France with the answer to the question of how chintz was created. After witnessing the process of dyeing the cotton chintz, de Beaulieu sent home to Paris

2 Public Record Office, Statutes at Large, vol. 5,1 George I to 2 George II, 1714 - 28/9, pp.338-40, 1768.

10

detailed letters to a chemist friend. Along with each letter, he sent actual samples of the chintz fabric during each stage of the process.   His letters and chintz samples can still be seen today - they are in the Musee' Nationale d' Histore Naturelle in Paris.

Another Frenchman, Father Coeurdoux also supplied his homeland with detailed step by step information of the intricate chintz process. In 1742, while trying to convert the Indians to Catholicism, Father Coeurdoux gained their trust and was supplied with insights into this long held Indian secret. Since the ban on chintz was still in effect at the time of Father Coeurdoux and de Beaulieu, French authorities felt publishing this information would be inconsequential. In 1759, when the ban was lifted, French and English cotton printers started producing their own chintz!

Chintz has always maintained a degree of popularity. During the 19th & 20th century chintz crossed over from the textile industry to wallpaper and pottery. The vibrant multi coloured floral designs have always delighted the consumer. England had become the leader in producing high quality chintz with the first 60 years of the 19th century being called "The Great Age of Chintz". They produced bold, brightly coloured naturalistic flowers. Switzerland, France and America produced chintz as well - but the designs tended to be smaller scale floral prints.

It was not uncommon for the designers working in the pottery studios to take inspiration from the popular textiles of the day. All the designers were well aware of chintz! It graced their homes in the form of draperies and upholstered fabric on sofas, covered their walls and was used to make ladies dresses. It was inevitable that chintz would find its way on to pottery as well.

Teapot Rating System

Throughout the book, you may notice a teapot icon. This is for the Teapot Rating System. A common easily found chintz pattern, would receive a rating of one teapot while the most rare have four or five teapots. I have also attached ratings to patterns applied to unusual shapes. For example, Maytime on a Dainty shaped cup is very rare and commands a five teapot rating.

The Teapot Rating System is not a price guide and not intended to affect prices of Shelley on the secondary market. The ratings reflect my own opinions and experiences. They also reflect geographical differences, since Shelley Pottery would export vast quantities of various designs to India or South Africa and not ship those same quantities to Canada.

"A true chintz is like a chintz curtain and also regarded as an all over floral pattern, even if its only one colour."

- September 1999,
Mr. Ray Reynolds former Manager
of Decorating at Shelley Pottery

Chapter 1
1 8 8 5 - 1 9 0 0

"To chintz or not to chintz,
that is the question…"

The Earliest Chintz?

Shelley Pottery produced thousands of different patterns on earthenware & bone china during their years in business. Most collectors today know of about 10 different chintz patterns. Actually, there are many, many more!

This book has been written using the original Shelley Pottery pattern books as a guide. What are the pattern books? Large, leather-bound old ledger books with cups hand drawn on the pages instead of the customary accountant's figures. It was impossible to commit to memory every different pattern produced by Shelley. To help employees correctly fabricate the extensive range of different patterns, the books were on hand as working tools, reference books and guides.

If an employee was in doubt as to how Pattern # 12679 should look, he simply checked in the pattern books. There he would find the pattern numbers listed in numerical order on the left-hand side of the page. He would also find a hand rendered drawing of a cup or sometimes a plate. The pattern books would show if the handle needed a solid colour or perhaps it was given a burnished gold treatment. It would tell how the foot should be shaded. Hand written notes were included next to the illustration of the cup. The employees had no doubt how to produce any pattern using this guide.

The pattern books were not the artists' concepts! Only production pieces appeared in the books. Unfortunately, we do not have the production records. These are lost to us. We do not know how many pieces of any one pattern were ever sold to the public. Some of the examples of chintz that follow are photos from these old Shelley Pattern books. Every effort was made to find real life examples, however, sometimes they could not be located.

The earliest examples of chintz seen in this first chapter, are monochromatic - only rendered in one colour. Are they a true chintz? Perhaps not. According to the earliest definitions of the textile chintz - it must be multi-coloured. If you were to ask a fabric person if these patterns are chintz they would give you a resounding "No". In these early days of decorating pottery with chintz patterns, it was very difficult to use multiple colours. As you will see, the transfer printing method was very involved and only produced one colour at a time!

Only the earliest chintz patterns were decorated using the transfer printing process. The designer's free hand original art work was given to the engraver who put the art work on a copper plate. Then the printer would apply ink to the copper plate, put thin tissue paper on the plate and run it through the press. Next, an employee aptly called a Transferer, took the tissue paper, cut the amount needed and then carefully placed the thin tissue paper face down on the ware. A stiff brush was used to rub down the tissue paper. The paper was then washed away leaving the outline of the flowers on the pottery. Finally the piece was sent to the kiln for firing. 🐾

Thistle
1 8 8 5 - 1 8 9 1

This chintz is a delightful pattern showing a bunch of Scotch Thistles with their stems & leaves. The pattern was produced using the transfer printing process. It was produced in six different colours: Blue, Rose, Brown, Bronze Green, Salmon, and a colour called Heliotrope.

The Thistle pattern was put on a variety of different shapes: Square, Victoria, Jubilee Flute, Alexandra, Albert and Daisy. Each time Thistle was put on a different shape or colour it was assigned a different pattern number.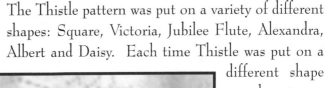

Thistle Pattern numbers:

#	Shape	Colour
#3544	Square	Blue Colour
#3545	Square	Rose
#3546	Square	Brown
#3547	Square	Bronze Green
#3576	Victoria	Solid Salmon all over
#3634	Jubilee Flute	
#3635	Jubilee Flute	
#3636	Jubilee Flute	
#4009	Alexandra	Heliotrope
#4010	Albert	Heliotrope
#4149	Alexandra	
	Daisy Shape	Blue

Blackberry
1885 - 1940

This is the next chintz design to appear in the pattern books, #3576 Blackberry. It must have been a favourite of the designers as it was used extensively. It was sometimes used in a solid colour with individual flowers, leaves or berries hand enameled in contrasting colours. Frequently, the pattern name changed when entered in the pattern books. Yet despite the numerous names used by Blackberry, it is the same charming design. Thorny stems, jagged serrated leaves and blossoms composed of 5 rounded petals are the dominate elements. If one looks closely along the stems, round berries emerge.

The Blackberry design is also called Bramble, Old Bramble Chintz, Gold Print and Gold Blossom. It is one of the few Wileman patterns to be used up until 1940. When Blackberry was first used in 1885, it was rendered in a single solid colour: Blue, Brown, Rose, Pink, Heliotrope and Electric Blue. It was put on different shapes: Victoria, Square, Worcester, Fairy and Albert.

When it was used in the later years, Shelley put it on the Ripon shape, Ely, Mocha and Gainsborough shaped cups. It was also used on Dainty and low Dainty shaped cups/saucers. A 1939 entry in the pattern books show the Blackberry pattern (called Gold Blossom Chintz) used on teapots and coffeepots too! ❧

Left, is a bold Electric Blue coloured Blackberry dish. Below, pattern #13217 shows individual flowers and leaves hand-enameled in bright colours.

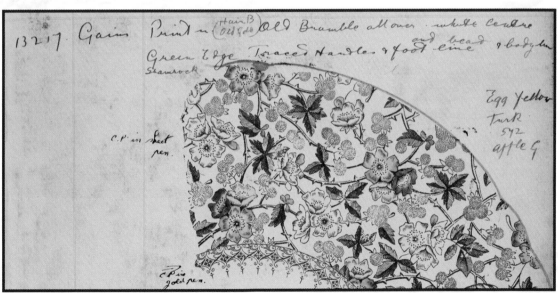

Clover
1 8 8 7

Pattern #3651 is the next monochromatic chintz to appear in the early pattern books. It is a single entry for a Jubilee Flute shaped cup & saucer. It is described as being rendered in all blue. There is no illustration of this chintz. There is never another mention of the Clover Chintz pattern!

The cup and saucer below is the only example of this rare chintz known to be in existence. As you can see, it is a tiny scale chintz showing a round clover type blossom with trailing stems and heart shaped leaves. It is a fairly dense chintz.

Dolly Varden
1887 - 1891

Dolly Varden (pattern #3744) where did they get this name? The artist who designed this chintz had a very painterly style. It has a much more relaxed feel to it than other designs. The artist was obviously not concerned about producing a botanically correct rendering, as leaves gracefully bend on lax stems. It favours stylized daisy blossoms, some with ragged, jagged edges and some merely lance shaped. Round buttercup type flowers many without any stems, float in the air! The whole scene is a profusion of garden flowers.

What the designer has done next to these flowers is quite interesting. He has rendered in reverse a very dense repeating geometric pattern. Very little of the white background colour shows through this reverse. It is predominately blue (or whatever colour the pattern was printed in!) and creates a nice design tension between the casual languid flowers and the tightly drawn pattern.

Dolly Varden was produced in eleven different colours: Blue, Pink, Brown, Bronze Green no.35, Pearl Grey, Sevres Green, Electric Blue, Heliotrope, Golden Brown, Silver Grey, and Golden Green.

Despite the wide range of colours used in the Dolly Varden pattern, it was only put on two different shapes, the Alexandra and the Worcester. 🌸

Jungle Sheet
1889 - 1894

This pattern is so close to Jungle Print, it is almost impossible to tell the difference. The only difference I can see is that Jungle Sheet is not quite as dense and has a little more of the white background showing through. It is missing some of the buttercup and pansy outlined designs behind the more pronounced daisy and asters.

It was put on the Daisy shape, the Fairy shape, Lily and Victoria shape as well as on the Albert coffee.

Jungle Sheet was produced in numerous colours and often found listed in the Seconds pattern book:

Blue, Red, Electric Blue, Pink, Dove, Golden Brown, Heliotrope, Lily Blue, Victoria Blue, Brown, Sevres Green, Bronze Green, Pearl Grey, Silver Grey, Golden Green, and Purple! This is the first time we see the colour Purple mentioned in the pattern books. 🐾

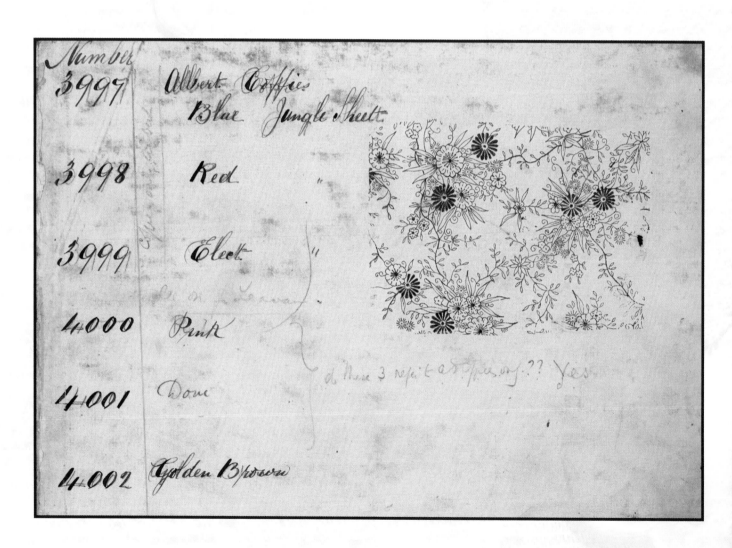

Jungle Print
1 8 9 1 - 1 9 4 0

This is a very, very dense chintz pattern. Jungle Print, #4148 is literally covered with the outline of daisies. The center of each daisy is a solid dot of colour. Smaller buttercup and pansy blossom contour lines are hiding in amongst the stems and leaves. This outlined design does not use any shading. Some of the larger Asters are solid in colour instead of being rendered in an outline. These few solid Asters make a wonderful contrast to the majority of this line drawing chintz pattern. It's ironic that none of these flowers would actual live in a tropical jungle! Perhaps the name was intended to convey a 'jungle' of flowers?

What I also found next to the Jungle Print pattern is a section of Cloisello pattern. This is clearly a separate piece of thin tissue paper being used to lay the Cloisello pattern down on the ware. Look closely, there is a heavy line of excess ink where the Jungle Print and Cloisello meet. Cloisello doesn't make its way into the pattern books until 1916, yet there it is, or a very close relative. Cloisello is a reverse pattern with very little of the white background colour allowed to show through. The pattern is made up of circular swirls on a shaded background. On top of the swirls are flowers. Some have 5 petals and some having 9 petals. At the end of each petal is a dot of colour.

The line drawing of the flowers works very well next to the few sections of the dense reverse Cloisello pattern. This same technique was first used in Dolly Varden. I would guess that the same designer who created Dolly Varden also designed Jungle Print.

Jungle Print was put on the Alexandra, Lily and Fairy shape. In 1940 , Jungle Print re-emerges as pattern # 13190. It was applied to the Ripon, Gainsborough, and Mocha shapes and the Cambridge coffeepot. It was produced in Blue, Electric Blue, and Red. 🌣

Snow Drop
1 8 9 9 - 1 9 0 0

This is a delightful chintz pattern that features the graceful nodding heads of the Winter blooming white bulb Galanthus, or commonly called "Snowdrop." The artist who designed Snowdrop must have been a gardener as well. The rendering of the Galanthus is very accurate showing the narrow strap-shaped basal leaves and the long thin stems bent over under the weight of the white flowers.

Snowdrop was only ever produced on the Daisy shape, but in many, many different colours:

Blue, Pink, Brown, Sevres Green, Bronze Green, Pearl Grey, Red, Heliotrope, Golden Brown, Electric Blue, Silver Grey, Golden Green, Salmon, Spring Green, Dark Grey, and Apple Green.

The Backstamp

These earliest chintz patterns in this chapter, do not carry the familiar Shelley backstamp, some collectors refer to these as "pre-Shelley". Originally, Shelley Potteries was known as Wileman & Company. These early chintz pieces bear the backstamp showing the entwined letter "W" and "C" which stands for Wileman & Company. Joseph Shelley became a partner in the business with James Wileman in 1872. The name Wileman & Co would remain for the next 50 years, even though Mr. Wileman left the business in 1884.

In 1881 Joseph Shelley's son, Percy Shelley joined the company. It wasn't until 1910 that the company adopted the trademark Shelley China. The business becomes a 'family affair' in 1918 when Percy Shelley's three sons, Bob, Jack and Norman went to work at the Pottery.

1872-90

1890-1910

1910-25

1925-40

1940-66

1940-66

- 1860   Foley China Works built in a region between the towns of Longton & Fenton UK which is known as The Foley.
- 1862   Joseph Shelley joins the company.
- 1872   J.F. Wileman makes Joseph Shelley a partner - the new company name is Wileman & Co.
- 1881   Percy Shelley joins the business. Percy is the son of Joseph Shelley
- 1884   James Wileman leaves the firm.
- 1896   Joseph Shelley dies, leaving Percy who is now 36 years old in control.
- 1910   The trade name is changed from Foley China to Shelley China. The backstamp showing the name Shelley inside a shield is developed. The words "Late Foley" are also incorporated.
- 1912   The Oleander shape was introduced - it continues to be a success today!
- 1918   Percy Shelleys' three sons join the company. Percy Norman is 19 and the twins, Vincent Bob and Kenneth Jack are 18 years old.

"Chintz – a potent
symbol of the new,
confident Bourgeoisie
of the British Empire
to show that they
had arrived with
style and panache."

- Paul Hutton,
UK and USA Antiques dealer

Chapter 2
The Early 1900's

Auto Teapot, 12s. (2pts). Lithographed Jacobean all over cover
also. & Gilt

7851

Auto. Teapot 12s ((2pts)). Lithographed. Fentons Large Rose Chintz
also on cover. Gilt

Auto Teapots
1 9 1 3

In one of the oldest surviving pattern books, dated February 28, 1913, I spotted these two images of teapots covered in chintz patterns. They are multi-colour, they are most definitely floral designs and they are applied all over the ware, including the spout of the first teapot! They have no name assigned to them - just the pattern numbers.

We see that the decoration is not produced by using a transfer printing method. It is obvious that this chintz was not made using a line drawing from a copper plate, as all the previous chintz patterns were produced! These chintz patterns were produced using a lithograph.

What exactly is a lithograph? The word "litho" is Greek for stone, while the "graphein" means to write. Lithography is basically a printing process using a stone or metal plate and ink to produce an image. For economic reasons lithographic printing soon replaced the engraving and transfer method, by the 1920's and early 1930's it is the predominate method used at Shelley.

A ceramic transfer company would make lithos using special pigments, metallic oxides, that can withstand the heat of the kilns. The process begins with a piece of Duplex paper coated with varnish. While the varnish is still sticky, the paper goes through a dusting machine that puts on a fine coat of metallic oxides. The loose pigment dust is removed and the paper is left to dry for twenty four hours. Only one colour per day can be applied to the paper, so the litho for Auto Teapot #7850 would take five days to create.

Of these metallic oxide colours, maroon and pink are the most expensive to use since they are derived from real gold. The colour red is made from ferrous oxide, green from chrome and blue from cobalt. When the litho was used it was placed upside down on the clay body. A special gum layer attached to the litho sheet helps it adhere to the ceramics.

Auto Teapots were given that name because of the additional piece that would sit inside the teapot holding the tea leaves! It was shaped like a cylinder and had many small holes to allow for the hot water to mingle with the tea. Quite a clever idea! These stunning teapots have no official name, just a number:

7850   *Auto Teapot, 12's (2 pts) Lithographed Jacobean all over, cover also & Gilt*

This chintz is very bold & sassy! The large pink & red Dahlia's are anything but timid. This litho uses five different colours: black for the thorny stems, light and dark green for the leaves and finally red and pink on the Dahlia. What is unusual in this teapot is having the litho applied to the spout. All the chintz teapots produced after 1923 have no litho on the spout or handle.

7851   *Auto Teapot 12's (2 pts) Lithographed Teutons Large Rose Chintz also on cover. Gilt*

This chintz litho uses even more colours. Light pink, dark pink roses, light and dark green leaves, light and dark shades of blue on the Morning Glories, light & dark yellow on the daisy like flowers, and a wonderful black dot stippled background! An absolutely stunning pattern. I'm not sure what the word "Teutons" means in the pattern book, it could be a reference to a lithograph maker or perhaps it is a variety of rose? 🐛

Cloisello
1913-1916

This pattern was produced on both bone china and earthenware. It was originally called Daisies back in 1913 on pattern # 7919. It features an underglaze in blue with a white Daisy on top. No leaves or stems. Nothing realistic about this highly stylized daisy! The space between the daisies is filled with a hand drawn swirl line.

Once the blue underglaze was applied to the ware - the transfer printing method was used to obtain the daisy & swirl line design. The copper plates with the design etched on them would be inked up, tissue paper put on the plate and run through the press. Then the tissue paper was put on the ware.

Shelley produced a huge range of vases and bowls. Not quite so common is the wonderful Tulip shape teapot shown below.

An interesting discovery for me in the pattern books late in 1916, Cloisello appears again, but this time the individual flowers are enameled in blue, yellow and red! The outlines of the flowers and the background swirls are black. It's pattern #11271, shown on page 39. 🐦

🐦 *Usually found in the blue colourway and a very desirable pattern for collectors today.*

The bowl above is very, very large and makes a dramatic statement. The gold rim is in perfect condition!

The "ring holder" shown at right in quite an unusual piece. The owner uses this piece.

_____ _____ in { 5 - 649 apple Gn. }
                { 1 - Cromel yellow }
                { 1 - 487 Blue. }

_____ in Harrisons Pink, stems in ½ Black
+ ½ 1632 Brown, stencilled, then blown all over Black.
Bellum, lig gold finish.

Swansea Pattern. on White Earthenware Vases.

Printed on Bisque in Harrisons Matt Blue 1000.
Fired in the oven & Enamelled through Kiln
Vases only Lig Burnish Gold finish. other pots lig. gold

Swansea Lace
1 9 1 6 - 1 9 3 8

A delightful pattern with a black delicate lacy background which serves as a showcase for the bold pink & red Peonies. Small daisy type flowers are enameled in red, yellow and blue. This pattern was produced initially on earthenware vases.

What I like most about this pattern is the name. Swansea is a town in South Wales where lace production is the major economy! Swansea Lace is certainly worthy of its name with its background so intricate, fine and lacy in detail.

Swansea Lace patterns:

#7924	Produced on various Vases	
#8193		
#10876	Royal Shape	
#11301	Gainsborough Shape	
#11302	Gainsborough Shape	On purple ground on body
#12668	Cambridge Shape	1937
#12706	Chester Shape	1938
#12707	Cambridge	1938
#12708	Cambridge	1938

Swansea Lace is not commonly found in the United States. Collectors find it more often in the UK and Australia.

Chinese Peony
1 9 1 6

On January 22, 1916 the Chinese Peony pattern appeared in the Shelley Pattern Books as pattern number #8151, not long after Swansea Lace. It is almost identical to Swansea Lace, using the exact same lacy backdrop. The only real difference is the Peony flower itself, having fewer petals than the flowers in Swansea Lace.

We all grew up seeing the Peony in our grandmothers' garden. The Peony is a huge flower with 3 to 4 inch blooms with eight or more petals usually in white or pale pink. The foliage is dark green and lance shaped. These large shrubs have long been prized for their bold foliage and showy blooms! The fact that they live for 30 years or longer, when left undisturbed, is merely an added benefit.

The common garden Peony, or Paeonia, is a native to China. They were first brought to England in 1200 by plant hunters when they were considered an important healing herb. Plantsman of the seventeenth century considered Peonies to be a vital element in the garden. One such gardener John Rea (1681) demanded "great Tufts of the best Pionies'. . ." must be used when planting a garden fret.

Peonies with the double flowers are great cottage garden favourites, especially the bold red Paeonia officinalis 'Rubra Plena'. There are also double pink and double white forms of this species which originally came from southern Europe in the mid-sixteenth century. The Peony continued to be a main character in Victorian gardens, and is now starting to make a come back in our gardens.

Given how popular the Chinese Peony is in the typical English garden, it was inevitable that it would inspire a design at this time. The artist did a very good job showing the lance shaped foliage, but took some liberties with the blue colour of the blossom. What I find interesting in both Chinese Peony & Swansea Lace is that the designer shows the Daisy and the Peony growing on the same stem! Quite impossible - but a delightful pattern regardless. 🐾

Jan 22/ 16

8151   *Chinese Peony Deco, in Oreu blue as used for Cloisello on glazed white Earthenware. Fired through Glost - oven, then tinted in Blown colours, Liquid Gold Edge & Kiln.*

Chinese Peony Patterns:

8151   *used on earthenware   1916*
12467   *Oxford Shape   1935*

Jany 22nd/16
8151

Chinese Peony Deco. in oven Blue as used for Cloisello
or Glaze White Earthenware
Fired through Glost-oven, then tinted in
Blown Colors, Liq Gold Edge, &tile

11273

11274 Milton Litho Kankow; decoration as 11270
Ground 93 93½ Orange   or ref number
Black Edge Hdle & Lines

11275 Milton Litho Jacobean in 11270 style
939 Ground
Black Edge Hdle 2 Lines

Hankow
1 9 1 7

This chintz has a very exotic feel to it. The stylized turquoise blue and orange dragon dances among green leaves and orange lotus blossoms. Light blue swirls cover the background elevating the dragon from the confines of the ground and making it appear as if dancing in a dream. Look closely at those background swirls - they are the exact same swirls used in the background of Cloisello!

Can you see the Dragon? His mouth is open and obviously snarling at his enemy. His turquoise blue tongue is sticking out and a blue flame seems to be blowing out from his nose! He has 3 sharp pointed claws at the end of each foot. Quite a menacing sight!

When I first encountered this pattern, I was confused by the two different pattern names, Kankow and Hankow. Which one could it be? One had to be a typo. I was extremely lucky to have Mr. Ray Reynolds on hand to help me decipher his predecessors handwriting in these old pattern books. Mr. Reynolds was the Decorating Manager at Shelley from 1949 until 1966. Ray was certain that the intended name was Hankow. I agree with him and this is why.

Many of the Shelley names come to us directly from the villages scattered close to Stoke on Trent.

Considering this patterns' obvious oriental flavour it seems logical to have been named after a Chinese city. I could not find any city named Kankow in China or Japan. However, Hankow is quite a well known Chinese city!

Hankow lies along the Yangtze River and the smaller Han River. It is the fifth largest commercial city in China in the Hubei Province. Hankow became a major commercial center during the Sung Dynasty (960 - 1279). During the 18th Century, Britain had a Concession in Hankow.

This pattern is first mentioned in a pattern book dated 1911. The pattern appears after the date 11/1/17 and the entry is merely text. It says:

8209   Hankow Litho deco all over & edged in mixture
1. Brilliant Orange
2. No. 8 Flux
3. White enamel

The next entry in the pattern books is dated April 1, 1919.

11274   Milton Litho Kankow (Hankow) decoration as 11270. Ground 9393 1/2 Orange, Black Edge & handle & lines.

 I have never seen Hankow in the States and know of only one vase in the UK.

Jacobean Chintz
1 9 1 7

On the same page of the pattern book, just below Hankow is another wonderful chintz called Jacobean Chintz. It's pattern number #11275. I was so excited when I discovered this chintz in the pattern books, having never seen this pattern before! It has become one of my personal favourites. There are no clues as to why the name Jacobean was given to this floral pattern.

As you can see in the example from the pattern book shown below - Jacobean Chintz uses purple, red, blue Peonies, and smaller lavender Primulas with bold green leaves. The leaves have a light green line down the center showing the veins. There are also small clusters of yellow seeds with the foliage of the lavender

Primulas. The designer of this pattern has stylized the flowers quite a bit, in fact they may not be Peonies or Primulas at all!

11275   Milton   Litho Jacobean in 11270 style 9393 Ground Black Edge & Handle and 2 Lines

When the Pattern Book refers to applying this Jacobean Litho in the same manner as #11270, it means that the chintz litho is applied to the outer most 5/8" of a plate, and the very center 2 1/2 " will have chintz litho. The space between the outer rim and the center is a solid mustard yellow colour.

The cups have the litho applied to the inside! The exterior is the mustard yellow colour or the 9393 Ground colour and the handle is solid black.

I know of only one example of this chintz. I was thrilled when the owners consented to having it's picture taken for this book! It is actually a tiny little salt pot just an inch or two in total size and it has the Jacobean Chintz litho applied to the outside. 🍵

Considering how unusual it is to find Jacobean Chintz I would say it is extremely rare, and give it a four teapot rating. It would be wonderful to find this Jacobean Chintz pattern on a teacup or teapot!.

Cactus Sheet
1 9 1 7

Here is an unusual chintz pattern. It first appears as pattern number #11272 and doesn't have a name, just the mention of Cactus Sheet Print. This litho is applied to the inside of a Milton shaped cup. The outside being done in the 9393 orange yellow ground colour. The handle of the cup is solid black. There is a black line on the rim of the cup.

The notation states that this litho should be applied to plates in the same fashion as in pattern # 11270 which is shown opposite. It also states that the individual flowers are to be enameled as shown in the sketch. These flowers look like a Poinsettia, but instead of being red they are half black and half blue or pink!

In 1938 and '39 this same litho was applied in a single gold colour on a variety of both the Ripon and Dainty Shapes. ❧

Cactus Sheet Patterns:

#11272	Milton Shape	1917
#12848	Henley	1938
#12999		1939
#13255	Dainty Shape	1938
#13097	Ripon Shape	1939

🐦🐦 *Collectors rarely find this pattern. It has also been called Gold Print Chintz and Poinsettia Chintz.*

11270 Milton Cups & Slops. Print inside, Swansea lace
June/23 Ground lace outside 9393½ @ Orange &c. Black ^ Cudney &c.
Saucers Grounds only " " centre white
Muffins Print band and circle as sketch
Creams Printed band from edge to
Enam as Sketch shoulder. Ground below
Black E & Lines. BYB's as Muffins
Solid Black Hdle .... CENTRE
.... 2½ inches ....
5" ⅝ Tinted in
5 Purple.
Rose x x.
Yellow Grn
CREST GREEN

6 M Muffin
For
Size of centre
& Band

11271 Milton as 11270 but Daisy print in Hair
Enam as sketch.
Ground in 9393½
or by Ref Number

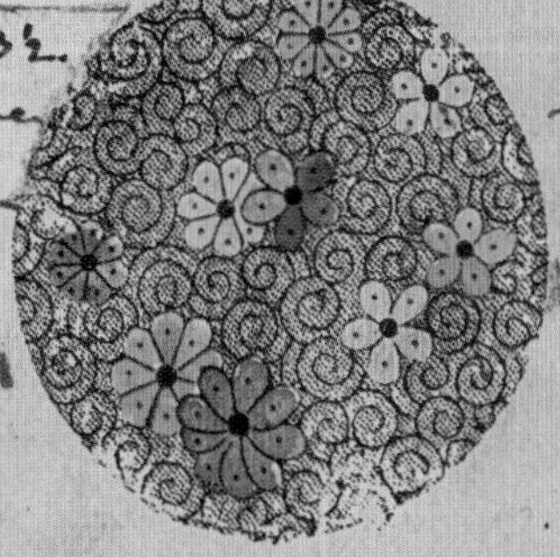

Tinted in
ENAM YELLOW
ROSE x x
TURKISH BLUE

11272 Milton as 11270 but Cactus Sheet print in 1632
Enam as Sketch. Ground in 9393½

Tinted in
ENAM YELLOW
ROSE x x
TURKISH BLUE
1365 Green

Blue Dragon
1 9 1 8

The next chintz pattern to appear in the pattern books is number #8315, the Blue Dragon. Blue Dragon appears quite regularly in the UK and Australia. Collectors find it much harder to obtain in the United States. Is it a true Chintz? Once again that will be up to the individual collector. It is an all over floral pattern, but is does not use multiple colours. In addition to flowers and butterflies, this design incorporates a dragon.

The dragon is much more realistic than the one used in Hankow. This dragon has scales on its snake-like body, spiky projections around its head and all along its body. Look carefully as sometimes it is difficult to see the dragon at first. 🦋

Black Dragon
1 9 1 8

Pattern number #8390 shows a Tulip shaped earthenware jug with the Dragon pattern. This entry in the pattern books called the litho "Black Dragon" instead of Blue Dragon! The breweriana, or 'bar furniture' jug was made for a client in Scotland. Notice the spelling of the word Whiskey, the Scottish version of the word has been used.

Can you see the dragon? Whether the pattern is called Blue or Black Dragon - he looks the same. He has a black face with large round white eyes and is lurking on the lower right-hand side of the whiskey jug.

8390   Tulip jug Oval Badge on each side "The Kind of Scotch Whisky" printed in U.G. Black Dragon all over in Japan Blue. Fired through oven "Jamie Stuart" printed in Blood Red on each side. Gilt in Liquid Gold.

🫖🫖🫖🫖🫖 *Highly collectible, impossible to find on teacups. Collectors rarely find this chintz. One is more likely to find it in Australia & New Zealand on bud vases and bowls. This Grape & Rose Chintz teapot is quite a magnificent find! I know of only one of them - and it's exquisite. As well as the previous Auto Teapot, pattern #7850 and #7851, this one has the chintz litho applied all over. It has the Grape & Rose Chintz on the handle and the spout. In the later years, Shelley stopped applying chintz to handles and spouts as it is a very difficult task to fold the chintz litho paper around a handle.*

Grape & Rose Chintz
1 9 1 8

This is a fantastic chintz pattern. It was first used in 1918 and entered into the pattern books as number #8300. A second entry into the pattern books on June 22, 1923 gave it pattern number #11276.

Unfortunately, it does not have an 'official' name. The Shelley pattern books simply call it a Chintz Litho. Clusters of black grapes with green leaves tinged pink hang on vines along with red Roses & large blue Peonies. Tiny yellow flowers appear randomly here and there clinging to the same vines. The space in between the vines is filled with little green swirly circles and groups of burgundy dots. Unlike other chintz patterns, this one has a black & white checker board pattern that runs along the top.

This litho was an uncontrolled pattern, which means that Shelley did not pay to have exclusive rights to it. The ceramic transfer manufacturer could sell this chintz litho to anyone of his choice. The American company Taylor, Smith & Taylor used Grape & Rose Chintz and Grimwades produced a limited range of pieces in the 1920's. The lesser known Staffordshire pottery Empire also used this chintz design. It has also been spotted in New Zealand on pieces with no backstamps. I have been told that author Muriel Miller first coined the name "Grape & Rose Chintz" when writing about Royal Winton, and collectors have continued to use the name. ❧

11276 Milton   *Litho Chintz as 11270 finish. Ground Celadon or by reference number, Black Edge, Handle and 2 lines. June/22/1923.*

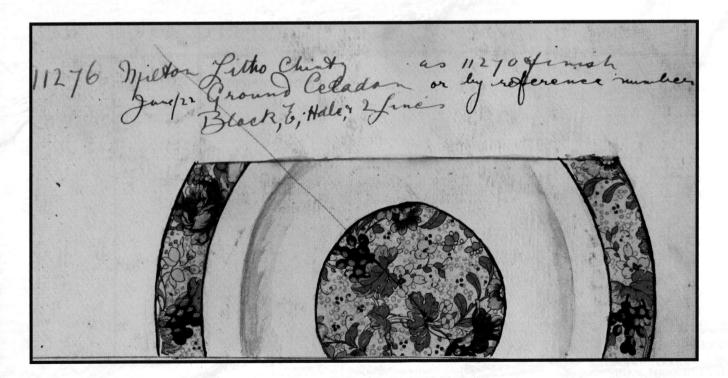

Cloisonne Pattern
1920 - 1938

Pattern number #8320 is assigned to the Cloisonne Pattern. I am not sure why Shelley used the word "Cloisonne" when describing this pattern. Cloisonne is the French word for 'partition'. It is a type of enamel work that uses thin strips of wired soldered on top of a metal plate. The space in between the wires is filled with different enamel colour.

I would guess that the name Cloisonne came from the background of this litho. If one imagines the white lines as being the metal strips and the black or blue background colour being the enamel - it does have a certain Cloisonne look to it. But the bold flowers on top of the crackle background look very realistic and not at all like a work of Cloisonne! What is interesting is that in the later years during 1938, this pattern name changes from Cloisonne to Crackle. 🍂

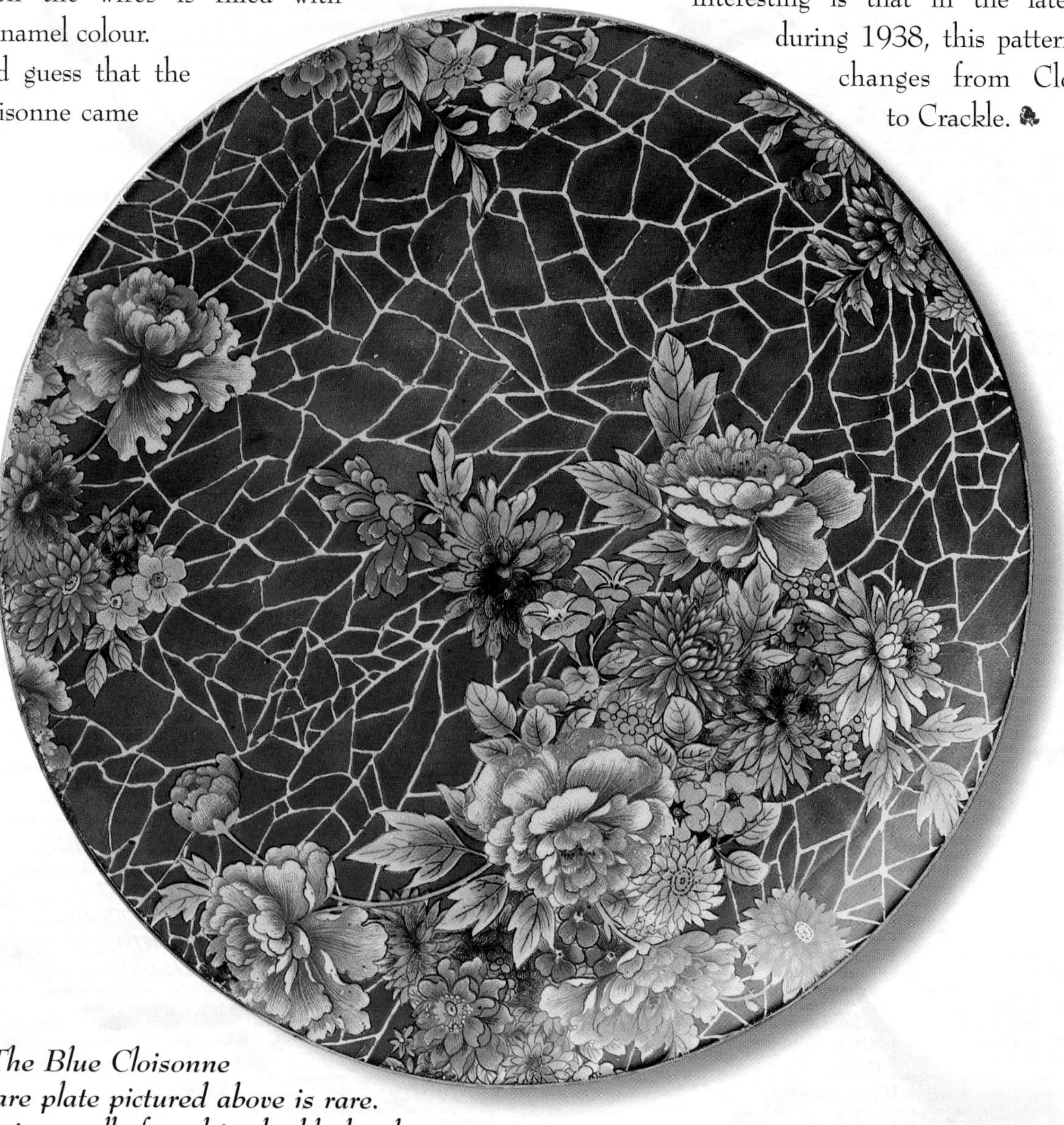

🍂🍂🍂 *The Blue Cloisonne earthenware plate pictured above is rare. Cloisonne is usually found in the black colourway. Expect to pay more for the blue version.*

🍵🍵 *A Mocha shaped cup & saucer, shown above. Below is the Ripon shape. Cloisonne is most commonly found in the UK and Australia. Rarely found in the United States!*

🍵🍵🍵🍵🍵 *This Queen Anne shaped Cloisonne is very, very rare. It will hold its value - a very good investment. A price tag of $300.00 or more for this trio would not surprise me.*

"Usable luxuries from a bygone era which are finite items that supply infinate pleasure. An heirloom investment that can only become more scarce & desirable."

- Andre van der Walt,

South Africa

Chapter 3
The 1930's - 1940's

Davies Chintz
1 9 3 5

Once again, Shelley neglected to give this chintz a name. Collectors refer to it as "Pink, Blue and Grey Leaves". This is a fairly uncommon chintz. It was produced in three different colourways only on bone china. The most commonly found colour being the pink, blue and grey combination. It was also produced with the same pink & blue flowers but with a bright green leaf. A third variation shows the flowers in yellow and green and the grey leaves.

James Davies was a ceramic litho manufacturer and they produced many of the patterns used by Shelley Pottery including a few chintz designs.

The Davies Chintz was put on a variety of shapes: Oxford, Regent (shown below), Princess Coffee, Cambridge and Ascot. ❧

🫖🫖🫖 *Very hard to find & expensive!*

Davies patterns:

#0118		
#0119		
#0120		
#2187	Oxford or Regent	(green & yellow colour)
#2188	Oxford or Regent	

#2189	Oxford or Regent
#2190	Princess Coffee
#12677	Cambridge and Ascot
#12678	Cambridge Square (pink, blue and green leaves)
#12679	(pink, blue and grey version)

Rose, Pansy, Forget-Me-Not Chintz
1 9 3 7

This is one of the loveliest chintz patterns that Shelley produced. It was first introduced in 1937 and continued until the 1950's. In fact, in 1950 when Ray Reynolds the Decorating Manager of Shelley was about to get married, Norman Shelley told Ray to pick out any teaset on the showroom floor as his wedding gift. Ray wanted the Rose Pansy Forget-Me-Not Chintz teaset more than anything else. He loved it, he thought it was the most beautiful set ever made! But, Ray's modesty didn't let him choose it. Mr. Reynolds said "We didn't have the nerve to ask for it as a wedding present." It was not only the most beautiful, but one of the most expensive sets Shelley ever produced! 🐞

The happy couple, Ray and Elsie Reynolds on their wedding day!

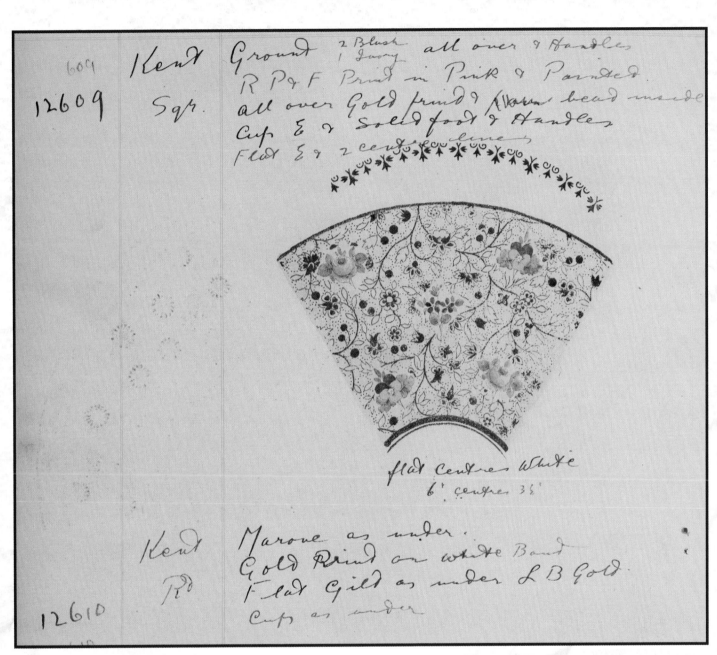

🫖🫖🫖🫖 *This is a very, very difficult chintz pattern to find. Not commonly seen in Australia or the United States. It has been found in Canada and the UK.*

Rose, Pansy, Forget-Me-Not chintz patterns:

#12609	*Kent Shape also Square Butter*
#12610	*Kent, Ripon and Gainsborough Shape*
#12612	*Kent and Ripon Shape*
#12712	*Chester shape*

#12717	*Chester shape, Blue colourway (blue groundlaid colour)*
#12718	*Chester shape, Ivory Wash all over background*
#12720	*Chester shape, Salmon Wash all over*
#12721	*543 Wash (543 is a pale green colour)*

The Process

One of the reasons for the high price tag on the Rose Pansy Forget-Me-Not chintz was the amount of labour involved in its production. Pattern #12609 was fired in the decorating kiln at least four times and possibly five. Each time a piece is fired there is a chance of something going awry - hence the high cost. Lets examine the steps necessary:

The process would begin by first printing from copper plates, the outline of the flowers in brown on to a printing tissue paper. This outline was transferred to the china by placing the paper face down on the ware. The paper was washed away leaving the outline of the flowers on the pottery. The piece was then sent to the kiln for firing.

After firing, the piece was sent to the groundlaying department. The groundlay was the background colour of the piece. In this pattern it was blue, ivory, salmon or pale green. The ground colour was applied by oiling the surface and then dusting the surface with a fine coloured powder. In those areas where other colours were to be later applied, as in the petals of the pansy, the ground dust had to be removed, by hand with a very pointed instrument. This would keep the colours pure & vibrant! If the ground colour was not carefully removed, it would taint the final colourings.

Again the ware was taken to the kiln to be fired. In the first years this pattern was produced, the next step was to take the piece to the enameling shop. Here the enamelers would meticulously hand paint each flower. A third firing would take place before the ware went for the addition of gold!

In the post war years the flowers were lithographed on - thereby saving a firing.

Now came the application of the delicate gold chintz leaf & stem design. The printing was done in the same manner as the first step for outlining the flowers. Copper plates with the stem designs would be covered in pure gold mixed with flux. Tissue paper was placed on the copper plates so that the design could be transferred to the ware. Once the paper was washed away leaving the gold design - it was fired again.

Finally the piece would make its way to the last department, the Gilding Department. Here it would have it's handles, rims and feet gilded. Once again it went to the kiln for a firing. After it came out of the kiln, the decorating process is still not quite finished - the gold which comes out of the kiln with a dull matte finish needs to be burnished or scoured with a fine round grained sand to achieve the final brilliant gold finish. This last step was all done by hand and very labor intensive.

During each step of this long process the ware would be inspected for faults. If a fault was found then the piece would be returned to the decorating department for correction or it would be completely rejected! Considering all the various steps involved and all the opportunities for mistakes - it is no wonder this was one of the most expensive chintz patterns to produce. Mr. Reynolds recalls that his favourite chintz pattern cost two or three weeks salary.

Here is a cup/saucer that utilizes ONLY the leaf & stem design portion of Rose Pansy Forget-Me-Not chintz. Instead of being rendered in gold here it is shown in green. The designers at Shelley chose not to add the individually hand enameled flowers. They also decided not to use a background colour, simply letting the white of the bone china provide contrast to the twisting jungle of green leaves & stems.

This is a simplified version of Rose Pansy Forget-Me-Not chintz and required only one trip to the kiln instead of four or five! Since the copper plates were already engraved with the leaf & stem design, it was easy to transfer this design onto the ware in any colour desired..

Ratauds Litho
1 9 3 8

This chintz design came from the design studio at Ratauds. Ratauds was one of the ceramic litho manufacturers in the Stoke area. They designed this lovely chintz in April of 1938. According to the archives at Ratauds, it was their pattern number 7585 and most likely only had a run of 1,000 sheets.

On June 27, 1938 this unknown chintz pattern was entered into the Shelley pattern books. This chintz appears to be designed to fit only the saucer edge and not the center of the saucer, where the cup would sit. One might call it a "Border Chintz". It is a lively combination of spring blossoms, pink Apple blossoms and blue Daffodils with bold green leaves and delicate grey fern sprays.

The Ratauds Chintz pattern was put on the Chester shape and the Cambridge shape. ❧

12780	Chester Cambridge	Ratauds Litho Liquid Gold Edge 1/4 handle
12781	Chester Cambridge	Ratauds Litho on Ivory size. Liquid Gold Edge 1/4 handle, Cambridge body & foot line. Plates Ivory to shoulder, Saucers to centre. Cups, Cambridge all over. Chester white well.

Having searched high & low for this Ratauds border chintz, I could find NO example, anywhere! I find it impossible to assign teapots.

THE FACES OF SHELLEY

Behind these wonderful cups & saucers that collectors cherish are many talented individuals. Girls who worked doing the free hand enameling, grinding & mixing colours, or in the gilding department. Girls who worked in the printing department applying the lithographs, spray painting or doing the painting of lines, swirls and petals.

These are some of the faces behind the Shelley that we covet today! This photo shows some of the girls from the 1930's: (back row left to right) Laura Chell, Ruth Rennie, Milly Bowen, Hannah Booth, Vicky Williams, Doris Chell and Ida Sheldon. (front row) Elsie Brough, unknown, Nancy Booth

12780 Chester Ratauds Litho. Ligs Gold Edge & Handle
Camber

12781 Chester Ratauds Litho on Ivory Size.
Camber Lig Gold & ¼ Handle Body & foot lines
Plates Ivory to Shoulder Sea to centre Cup &
Camber, all over Chester white well.

Flowers & Swirls Chintz
1 9 3 8

Flowers & Swirls is the only appropriate name for this pattern. It has no name mentioned in the pattern books. At this point in time, Shelley Potteries is now using more lithographs to decorate the wares, occasionally they would use the old print and enamel method. The print and enamel process was previously described, where a design is on a copper plate and transferred to the ware by using thin tissue paper. The individual colours are hand enamelled. This chintz is one of the last to use the print & enamel method.

The swirl design is not new. Look closely - it is the same background that Cloisello and Hankow used. On top of the swirl motif the designers have put a single flower on a stem with a leaf. Some of the single flower blossoms are left white, some are enamelled in Egg Yellow, Turkish Blue, and the leaves are Apple Green.

Another version of this pattern has all the flower blossoms left white and only the centers enamelled!

Sometimes the swirl background was printed in black, brown or gold. It was tried on a variety of shapes: Ascot, Henley and Ripon. On pattern #13001 there is mention of Teapots and Coffeepot printed in gold.

Not a very common pattern or one that collectors seem driven to find.

Flowers & Swirls patterns:

#12819	*Ascot shape*	*(background printed in black flux)*
#12820	*Henley shape*	
#12821	*Ascot shape*	
#13001	*Ripon shape*	*(Flower outlines & swirls done in gold) 1939 Teapots and Coffeepots*

820
12820 Henley   Print (Ham B) all over Enan 572. Tuck, Egg apple.
               (Old G)
        Sqr.   Liq Gold. Cups as 12821

12821   Ascot Autumn Print & Ena. Coral & Ginger
               L.G. finish as under.

Maytime Chintz
1 9 3 8 - 1 9 6 6

On February 1, 1938 Maytime Chintz was entered into the Shelley pattern books. This is one of the most popular chintz patterns that Shelley ever produced! Customers loved it just as much in 1938 as they do now. It was put on earthenware and bone china. It was applied to just about ever different cup shape available, and in virtually unlimited combina-

tions! Maytime was put on wall pockets, candlesticks, toast racks, juicers & condiment sets. It was put on lamps with matching lamp shades.

Maytime is aptly named. It features a cluster of Apple blossoms in various shades of pink & red among brown branches and green leaves. A few burgundy flower buds are shown next to flowers fully open.

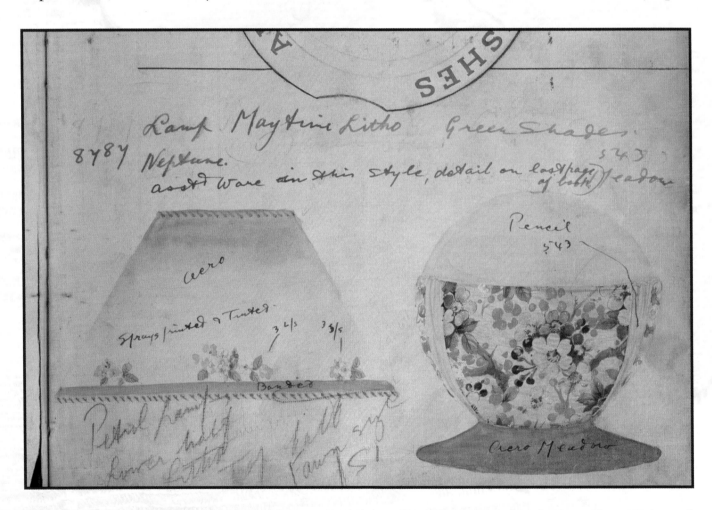

🫖🫖🫖 *Extraordinary - Maytime Chintz on a lamp! I have never had the pleasure of seeing one of these in person, but hear rumors of their existence. I do know that they were produced on earthenware with matching lamp shapes. The small cluster of Apple blossoms on the lamp shade duplicating the Maytime pattern is a nice design touch. If you come across one of these . . . BUY IT!*

Pictured above is Maytime Chintz, pattern #13452, on the classic Henley shape! Notice how the chintz litho is not applied to the teapot handle, knob or spout. It was extremely difficult to apply the litho paper to curved and rounded forms. Most of the chintz teapots produced by Shelley will be decorated in this manner, sans chintz on handles, knobs or spouts. It is the rare exception to find a decorated spout or handle!

Take a close look at the upper most teacup. Do you see that the Maytime pattern does not cover the entire cup body? The designers at Shelley Potteries employed countless combinations of decoration. This cup has a band of Maytime along the top half of the cup body and a soft pale cream colour used on the bottom. The handle is also a departure from the usual Henley shaped Maytime cup. Note the bottom half is cream while the top is white with a delicate gold trace pattern. This cup is pattern #13368.

Maytime is a small scale pattern that is fairly dense. Only a tiny bit of white background shows through. It is a wonderful chintz that reminds us of Spring.

Maytime was put on many different shapes: Empire, Oxford, Cambridge, Chester, Dainty, Henley, Ely, Ripon, Footed Oleander, and Boston. It was also put on the Canterbury and Westminster miniature shapes. Maytime can be found on various teapots and coffeepots.

The Maytime Chintz litho was the first one to be applied to the Footed Oleander shape!

Maytime's popularity continued to exceed that of other chintz patterns. The records at Capper-Ratauds show that in March of 1966, Shelley Potteries Ltd. order 1500 sheets of Maytime. This is far more than any other chintz pattern.

Maytime on an Ely shape, below, with a floral cluster inside the cup, have any of these survived?

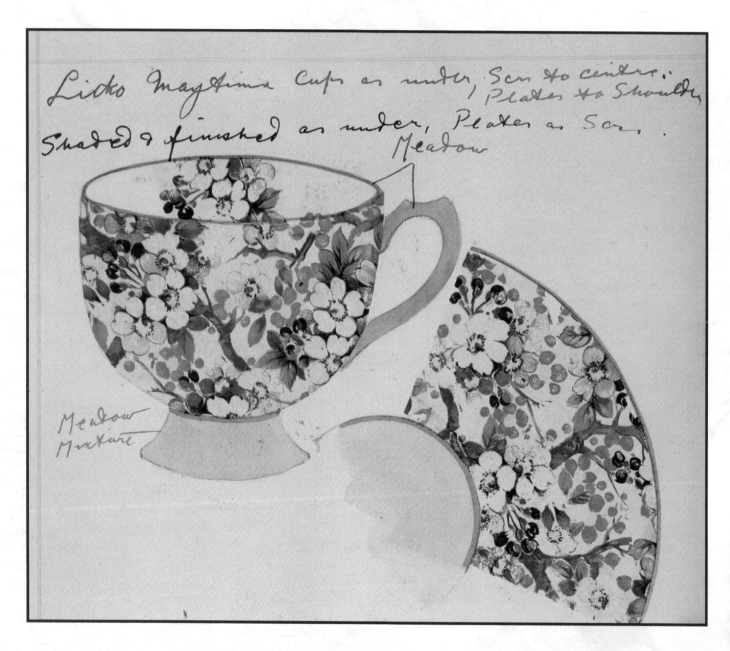

Here we see Maytime, pattern #13408 with a dramatic matte black exterior and the chintz litho applied to the inside of the cup! Very scarce. What is not obvious from the photo, the center of the saucer where the cup rests also has the Maytime design. The burnished gold handle, rim and foot make a bold contrast with the matte black colour.

Below is an unusual piece - a Juicer! This is pattern #8787. It is made in two separate pieces, the top section is the fluted reamer which is used for squeezing the juice from lemons or oranges. There are holes in the bottom of the reamer to catch the liquids, while the bottom piece has a spout and handle. The pale green colour used on the reamer is the perfect compliment to the Maytime's palette of predominantly pink & burgundy tones.

A Maytime Juicer is fairly rare, not something collectors will find readily.

Colour and trim variations add to the number of different pattern numbers, not just for Maytime but for all chintz patterns. Sometimes, when a pattern was applied to a new shape or in a different manner it was given a new pattern number . . . and sometimes Shelley didn't bother to assign a new number. 🍵

Maytime patterns:

#0105	Empire Shape	#972	Henley	#13368	Henley
#0106	Oxford Shape	#8787	Neptune Lamp	#13369	
#0107	Cambridge Shape	#8801	Vega Lamp	#13386	Ripon
#0108	Cambridge & Chester	#0708	Henley	#13408	Henley
		#12719	Cambridge	#13416	Footed Oleander
#0109	Chester	#12725	Chester	#13452	Henley & Cambridge
#0110	Chester	#12987	Ely Shape	#14175	Henley
#0114	Dainty Shape	#13020	Henley	#14215	Boston Shape
#0212	Chester	#13030	Chester	#14264	Ripon
#0395	Henley Shape	#13367	Ripon Shape		
		#13367	Footed Oleander		

🍵🍵 *The extremely popular Footed Oleander shaped cup & saucer shown above wearing Maytime Chintz on the inside. Footed Oleanders always have the pattern litho on the inside. This cup shape is the only one Shelley produced with the contours of flower petals impressed into the clay! The petal design, which is a soft pale pink, is on the outside of the cup and the top side of the saucer. This Maytime Chintz is pattern #13416.*

This earthenware Maytime honey pot has the same pattern number, #8787, as the Juicer shown on page 61. Sometimes when a pattern was applied to a different shape it would receive a different pattern number and sometimes not. Pattern #8787 was also used for the Maytime Neptune shaped lamp. I would guess that all earthenware pieces wearing Maytime have the pattern #8787. The honey pot measures 4" tall and over 3" wide, making it quite a large pot! The lid has a small notched opening to allow the handle of the spoon to extend out. The vivid green stem is a whimsical touch.

The apple shaped honey pot (shown right) covered in Maytime is not an easy piece to find. Expect to pay a premium if you discover one. I have seen prices starting at $250.00 and upwards.

The word "Ripon" comes from a town in the Yorkshire region of England, and it is well known for its cathedral. Using nearby village and towns to name various shapes was a common practice at Shelley Pottery.

Ripon shaped Maytime cups seem to be much harder to come by here in the States, when compared to Maytime Chintz on Henley and Footed Oleander! I rarely see Maytime on this elegant shape. It is one of my all time favourites.

Melody Chintz
1938 - 1963

Another popular success - Melody Chintz also appeared in the pattern books in 1938. It has a green background with tiny white jagged lines, almost too small for the eye to see. On top of the green background we find clusters of yellow Daisies, red & pink Daisies, and blue Daisies. Clusters of round puffy pink flowers that resemble Hydrangea are also part of this design. Stems with green leaves complete the decoration.

Melody Chintz was applied to both earthenware and bone china. It was applied on a wide variety of shapes: Cambridge, Chester, Henley, Ripon,

Footed Oleander, Boston, Richmond and Queen Anne. It was also put on the Gainsborough shape - but this is rarely found by collectors. It is shown in the pattern books on the extremely scarce Ely shape!

Melody patterns:

#0185	*Chester & Cambridge shape*
#0196	*Henley*
#0197	*Ripon*
#0209	*Cambridge*
#0210	*Henley*
#8815	*Neptune Lamp*
#12973	*Henley*
#12974	*Henley*
#13020	*Henley*
#13021	*Henley*
#13031	*Henley*
#13064	*Gainsborough*
#13105	*Henley (with red exterior)*
#13278	*Henley*
#13317	*Ripon & Henley*
#13331	*Oleander*
#13382	*Ripon*
#13412	*Footed Oleander*
#13453	*Henley*
#13594	*Henley*
#14076	*Richmond*
#14174	*Richmond*
#14210	*Boston shape*

Collectors today seek out this cozy chintz pattern. The Henley (shown left) and Ripon shape (shown right) are the most frequently found. Shapes like Chester, Boston and Gainsborough are less frequently seen and therefore command higher prices.

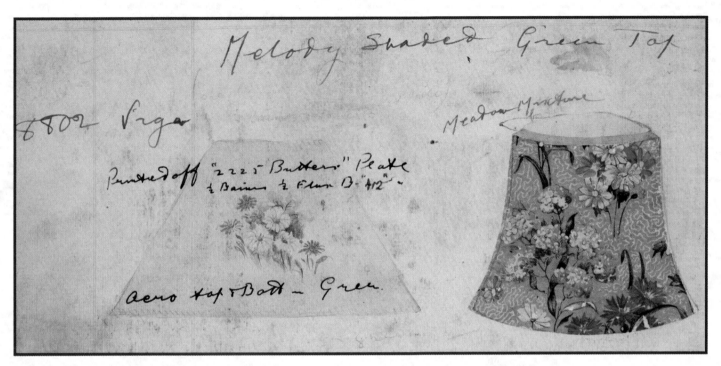

🫖🫖🫖🫖 *Melody was used on the Vega and Neptune style lamp, both made out of earthenware. A matching cluster of flowers from the Melody design was applied to the green lamp shade.*

This Melody Chintz teapot is in the Court shape, it is pattern #0185. The teapot has a white knob and white handle with delicate gold lines traced on top of the white colour. What is unusual is the application of Melody Chintz to the spout.

Shown here is Melody Chintz on a Chester shaped cup and saucer, it too has the pattern #0185. Notice how the designers applied the litho pattern to the inside of the cup while leaving the exterior white. The Chester shape is an easy one to identify, the handle will have a completely closed loop with two brackets attaching the loop to the cup body. Looks like a large ear sticking out of the cup! The saucer will also have a flange, or lip, at the very top.

🫖🫖🫖 *Although the Henley shape is one of the most common shapes, the cup at the right is most rare! A glossy cobalt blue exterior with the Melody Chintz on the interior - tres magnifique.*

The Melody cup with the cobalt blue exterior is glorious. The white handle makes a bold statement, and as we can see from the photo, the center of the saucer has the chintz litho as well. What a grand way to dress up a Henley cup. Once again, the designers at Shelley hit upon a successful combination.

Below is a page from the pattern books showing #13133 Melody Chintz on Ripon and Ely shapes. The Ely shape is almost never found by collectors today. Note the soft pale blue colour on the foot as well as the interior of the cup. The handle has been left white with delicate gold traced designs. The Melody pattern uses so many different colours, one could use any of them to accent, but I find the pale blue works very well. I doubt this cup would look as splendid if the rust or yellow colour was used.

🫖🫖🫖 *Melody Chintz applied to the Ely shape is exceptional.*

 *Another rare reverse combination. Melody Chintz on the inside and a saucy lime green exterior of a Henley shaped cup!*

🕊️🕊️ *Melody Chintz on the Gainsborough shape, it is pattern #13645. The Gainsborough shape is easy to spot with the distinctive graceful handle looping up taller than the rim of the cup! The Gainsborough cup has a foot which adds to the overall graceful look.*

🕊️🕊️🕊️ *Melody Chintz knife! What a rare piece. If you find one expect sticker shock when you learn the price.*

Rataud's New Chintz
1 9 3 9

On July the 24th of 1939 this chintz pattern was entered into the Shelley pattern books as #8833. It has no official name, just the mention that the chintz came from the ceramic lithograph company, Ratauds. This is a lovely chintz with both large and small scale flowers in a variety of colours, yellow, pink, red and blue. The leaves and stems are green. This is a very dense chintz with very little of the white background allowed to show through the design.

This chintz was applied only to the top half of the earthenware beaker.

What a pity that Shelley didn't produce cups/saucers, plates and a much wider range of tableware using this pattern! ❧

❧❧❧❧ *I could not find any Shelley chintz collector with an example of this pattern. It is a very bright & cheerful design. If you find it - buy it!*

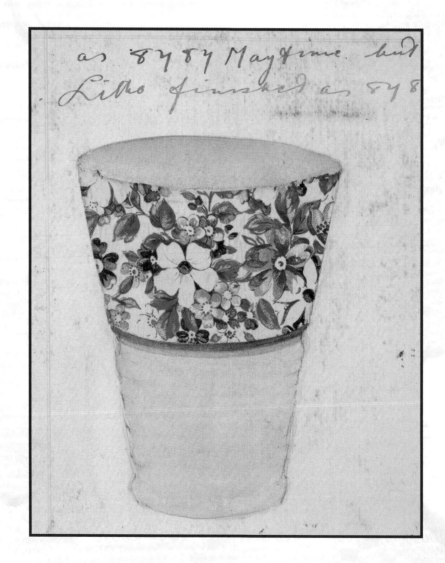

8833 " ass'd   as 8787 Maytime. but Rata and's New Chintz
Ware. Litho finished as 8787.

8834   ass'd   Blue & Daisy Litho (Rata and's) decorated
Fancy   as Melody. with Blue Bands, Shades
Ware

Rock Garden Chintz
1939 - 1964

Here we have a favourite with collectors, Rock Garden Chintz. Rock Garden is a very dense design. Instead of featuring various multi coloured flowers on a flat background, Rock Garden is an attempt at a more realistic garden scene. It actually shows a rock stepping stone path meandering through a garden. The garden is full of small alpine plants suitable for rock gardening. Alpine gardening is very popular with the English. Wander into any garden center in the UK, along with the annuals, perennials, seeds & trees there will always be a section on alpine plants! The artist who designed Rock Garden Chintz even added shadows beneath the plants to give a sense of depth. This pattern is absolutely delightful and appropriately named. Rock Garden uses a full range of colours: pink, blue, yellow, green, purple, white and brown.

It was applied to a wide range of shapes: Henley, Ripon, Oleander, Boston, Footed Oleander, Low Oleander, Victor and the Queen Anne shape. It was used on both Canterbury and Westminster miniature shapes.

Unlike Maytime and Melody, Rock Garden was never used on a lamp.

Rock Garden is one of the mainstays in the Shelley chintz world. Collectors love it and their love affair with this pattern never gives way to trends. It has consistently proved to be a chintz that people seek out and there appears to be a healthy quantity of Rock Garden in the marketplace. Rock Garden also maintains a healthy price tag! Here we see how elegantly the Ripon shaped cup shows off the Rock Garden Chintz pattern.

The earliest patterns are on earthenware. Rock Garden patterns:

#8836		#13353	Oleander	#13357	Low Oleander shape
#0396	Henley shape	#13354	Ripon shape		
#972/S63	Henley shape	#13355	Henley	#13359	Victor
#2293	Oleander dinnerware	#13356	Oleander	#13385	Ripon
				#13407	Henley

🍵🍵 *Rock Garden Chintz on the delicate Footed Olean-der shape, a superb combination. The pale pink exterior (shown above) is far more common than the one with the yellow exterior.*

🍵🍵🍵 *The yellow version of Rock Garden is ex-ception! The saucer is unusual, instead of apply-ing the pattern to only the center, the designers have put it on the outside Oleander petal section. The center is decorated with the yellow. It is very uncommon to find a yellow version of Rock Garden on the Footed Oleander.*

The Queen Anne shape was introduced in 1926, it was developed by Eric Slater who joined Shelley Potteries in 1919. Eric was a very talented artist, much like his father Walter Slater who supervised the design of patterns and shapes at the pottery. Author Robert Prescott-Walker is noted for saying "What seems to set Shelley apart . . . is that their wares captured the spirit of the age." The Queen Anne shape certainly captured the Art Deco spirit of the day!

The Queen Anne is an eight sided cup, four of the sides are wider than the remaining four with very sharp, hard edges. The handle is a triangle form. It is highly angular and geometric. Robert Prescott-Walker goes on to talk about diversity of design, inventive new shapes, willingness to embrace new ideas and styles of design. The Queen Anne shape is without a doubt creative.

The Queen Anne was a radical design departure from the traditional classic cup shapes. It was an enormous success in its time, with over 170 different patterns applied to it. The designs typically found on the Queen Anne are scenes of idyllic English cottages with flowers growing in a garden, Art Deco stylized trees bearing vivid fruit, or geometric patterns of floral swags. Rarely would one find an all over floral chintz pattern, such as this Rock Garden Chintz! ❧

A Queen Anne shaped cup & saucer covered in Rock Garden!! The word scarce does not begin to accurately describe it. This example was found hiding out in the wilds of Canada. I could not speculate as to a price tag on this one, but I'm certain it would be lavish.

🫖🫖 *A Rock Garden Chintz teapot in the Henley shape, elegant and refined. Teapots in general, are more difficult to locate than cup & saucers. And to find one without cracks in the lid or chips on the spout is a treat. Expect to pay $500.00 or more.*

A group outing at the St. Andrews Church carnival in Longton Park, England. The church is long since gone but not the memories, as Joyce Dillon (nee Perry) recalls her days at Shelley! Joyce Dillon is shown in the photo standing in the back row on the right holding a small child, her daughter Katherine Kavanagh. She was taken on at Shelley Potteries and trained as a lithographer, but she did not enjoy the work. She says she recalls the Shelley factory as being airy, light and up-to-date with all the latest regulations in the industry. Joyce Dillon's mother, also a Shelley pottery worker is standing furthest on the left.

Blue Daisy & Green Daisy
1 9 3 9

This chintz has either a blue background or green background to highlight the bold white Daisy. The Daisy Chintz pattern is a fairly large scale chintz. There are no other flowers in the design, only the stems and tiny leaves of the Daisy. Gardeners will recognize the flower as being the Summer blooming Chrysanthemum maximum. The artist has added some black shadows behind the white Daisy petals to make the Daisy stand out in a bold fashion.

The first examples of Blue Daisy and Green Daisy are on earthenware pieces. Shelley Pottery was in the process of closing down the earthenware works and soon all chintz patterns would only be applied to fine bone china.

Blue Daisy & Green Daisy can be found on a medley of shapes: Henley, Dainty, Cambridge, Chester, Kent, Dorothy, Ripon, Ely, Oleander and Footed Oleander as well as Boston. We are very lucky to have an example of Green Daisy in the Ely shape shown on the page opposite.

Collectors can find this chintz in Australia New Zealand, Canada, South Africa and the United States. It does not seem readily available in the UK. For whatever reason, this chintz pattern is not very popular today. This lack of demand for this pattern keeps the price relatively low. The exceptions being the unusual reverse combination! ❧

The Ely shaped Green Daisy cup, shown opposite, valuable due to its rare shape.

Here, once again, Shelley has used a reverse combination on the Henley shaped cup. The glossy cobalt blue exterior is certainly bold, while the Blue Daisy Chintz, with it vast amount of white colour, on the inside is a strong contrast to the exterior. Not as desirable as other reverse chintz combinations.

Blue Daisy & Green Daisy patterns:

#8834	Earthenware beaker	#13316	Ripon and Henley
#8835	Earthenware	#13332	Oleander
#13178	Dainty shape	#13333	Oleander
#13202	Henley shape	#13358/S	Ripon
#13203	Cambridge shape	#13383/S	Ripon
#13204	Ripon and Ely shape	#13384/S	Ripon
#13205	Henley	#13413/S	Footed Oleander
#13206	Cambridge and Dorothy	#13414/S	Footed Oleander
#13207	Ely and Ripon shape	#13450	Henley and Cambridge
#13279	Henley	#13451	Henley and Cambridge
#13280	Henley and Cambridge shape	#14210	Boston
#13284	Dainty	#14212	Boston
#13308	Henley and Cambridge	#14216	Boston
#13315	Ripon and Henley shape	#14268	Ripon
		#14269	Ripon
		#14272	Ripon

Without an effective front office taking care of business, customers would never know the great beauty that is Shelley. Filing orders, mailing invoices, taking care of payroll, sending out colour illustrations of the latest designs - these ladies did it all. As you can see, they are posing in front of the Shelley factory entrance. The Shelley sign is partially visible in the top right hand corner of the photograph.

Standing in the back from left to right we have: Eileen Corcoran who was secretary to Norman Shelley, Pauline Bishop a short-hand typist, and Margaret Critchlow also a shorthand typist. The two ladies in the front are Gladys Wall, on the left, a Senior wage clerk and Barbara Smith, right, the assistant clerk.

Although Green Daisy & Blue Daisy are not the most popular chintz patterns in the china cupboard, when applied to an uncommon shape, as with any chintz pattern, their value increases. That is certainly the case here with this fabulous Dorothy shaped cup & saucer. Rarely does one find a Dorothy shaped cup, in any pattern! This one was unearthed on the California coast. I was extremely happy that it journeyed East to sit for the photographer.

13407   Henley Ground outside & on flat
         Rock Garden inside & on Sci centres
         L B Gold Solid Handle foot & Edge
              Handle Tails are coloured.

Gold Tracing
on Coloured Handle.
except Black.

13408   Henley   as 13407 but Maytime

on Shoulders only Lined in Centre

13409   Henley as 13407 but Ivory Summer Glory

13410   Henley as 13407 but Pink Summer Glory

"Chintz to me is like bringing a garden indoors. The things of nature are a balm for life, whether they calm us, make us smile or bring us cheer."

- Anji Davis,
Former President of the National
Shelley China Club

Chapter 4
The Final Years
1940-1966

Blue Pansy Chintz
1 9 4 0

The pattern number #13165 entered into the pattern books in 1940. It is called Blue Pansy Chintz. Blue Pansy was created by the artists at ceramic lithograph maker Rataud's. This is an uncontrolled pattern and was used by many different Potteries, not just Shelley. Gibsons, Hollinshead & Kirkham, Ltd., Lord Nelson, Royal Albert and Sampson Smith, Crown Clarence Pottery, Ford & Sons as well as the Japanese all successfully used the Blue Pansy Chintz pattern.

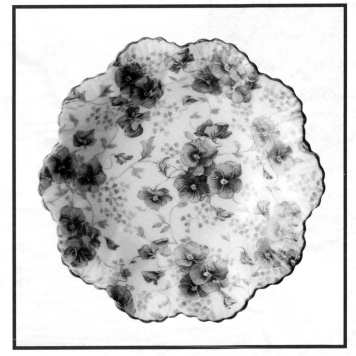

design. Blue Pansy Chintz is sought after by collectors. Shelley did not produce many pieces with the Blue Pansy Chintz design compared to their other chintz patterns, putting it very much in demand.

Blue Pansy Chintz can be found on the Henley shape, Ely shape, Footed Oleander, Ripon and Boston shape. ❧

Blue Pansy Chintz does not use as many different colours as other chintz patterns. Light blue, dark blue and a lime green. That's it - just three colours. There is quite a vast amount of white background behind the Pansies, this isn't a very dense

Blue Pansy Chintz is a very popular pattern with collectors. Even though it is one of the uncontrolled patterns, and can be found on ware made by many different makers, people still love this chintz. The sweet dish shown here is delightful, and not easy to find! I would expect to pay $100.00 or more for this dish.

Left, is a Shelley Blue Pansy Chintz teapot! Teapots were produced in much smaller quantities than just about anything else at Shelley. This lack of teapots pushes the value sky high. The teapot shown opposite is absolutely breathtaking. Its pattern #8831 and its in the Tulip shape.

Customers could buy a wide range of tea sets, dinner sets, breakfast sets, etc. from Shelley. When a customer bought a tea set it did not include the teapot. This may seem strange to us today, but at the time these were sold, tea sets were very dear indeed. Owning a Shelley bone china tea set was synonymous with good taste, refinement and elegance. It was thought that if one could afford a Shelley tea set that the customer would use their own silver teapot. Hence, teapots were sold separately.

A Blue Pansy Chintz Juicer, very unique. I would expect to pay $300.00 or more for such a piece.

Below we see a stack of Blue Pansy Chintz cups in the Henley shape. The soft blue handle and foot are the perfect compliment to the colours of the Pansy flower blossoms.

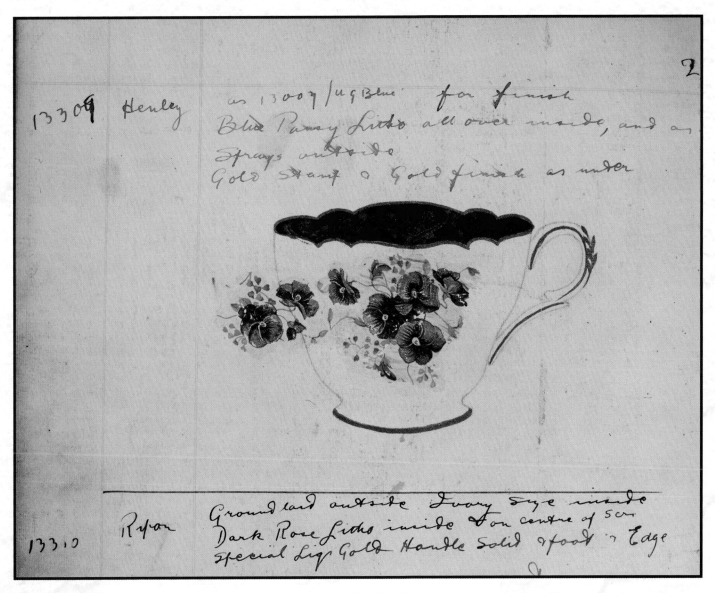

13309   Henley   As done in 13007/ U G Blue for finish. Blue Pansy Litho all over inside, and as sprays outside. Gold stamped border & Gold finish as under.

I've never seen an actual example of this Blue Pansy Chintz cup. I can only imagine how breathtaking it must be, with the pansy litho on this inside as well as some sprays on the outside!

Blue Pansy patterns:

		#14071	Footed Oleander
		#14218	Boston
#8831	Earthenware	#14230	Ripon
#13165	Henley shape	#14266	Ripon
#13166	Ely shape	#2489	
#13309	Henley	#0398	Henley
#14070	Henley	975/S47	Henley

🫖🫖🫖   *Collectors seek out these rare reverse combinations. Very few of them have been located, so prices have escalated beyond belief. Here we have a cobalt blue exterior with the Blue Pansy Chintz litho on the inside! A dramatic look on the Henley shaped cup. Recently on eBAY, the internet auction venue, a trio in this reverse cobalt combination sold for over $500.00.*

🫖🫖🫖 Here is a Footed Oleander cup with the Blue Pansy Chintz litho. The outside of the cup is done in a soft, pale blue. This soft blue accent colour completely changes the entire feel of the cup. Compare this one to the reverse shown on the opposite page. This Footed Oleander is delicate, gentle, soft & demure - quite feminine in overall character.

🫖🫖🫖 Right, is a Ripon shaped cup in the Blue Pansy Chintz, quite sophisticated. These are so hard to find - Prices for this cup would be $250.00 - $300.00 or possibly more.

Summer Glory
1 9 4 0

This is one of the most popular of the Shelley chintz patterns, and was produced in two different colourways, pink and yellow. When the yellow version of Summer Glory was entered into the pattern books it was always referred to as "Ivory" Summer Glory, yet the background is clearly yellow.

Summer Glory is an excellent name for this chintz, since it consists of Summer blooming Hydrangeas. This pattern is fairly dense with some of the background colour showing through. The Hydrangea clusters are rendered in shades of pink, blue and white among lush green leaves & stems.

Summer Glory was not used on as many different shapes as most other chintz patterns. It was only applied to: Henley, Cambridge, Ripon, Oleander and Footed Oleander shapes. Less frequently collectors will find Summer Glory on the eight-sided Queen Anne shape!

A few collectors will refer to the Pink Summer Glory as "Pink Clover". Shelley never called this chintz by this name. There is no mention of this name in any entry in the pattern books. Mr. Ray Reynolds, the Manager of Decoration says, "As far as I can remember we never put the Pink Clover name next to the backstamp".

In 1951, an importer/distributor in New York City called, The Edward Walker Company, who sold Shelley china, invented the name Pink Clover in their sales brochures. In the 60's, The Edward Walker Company changed its name to Shelley-Walker Ltd. 🍵

🍵🍵🍵 *Yellow Summer Glory will always command a high price. It is very desirable among collectors in both the yellow and pink colourway. Shown above is a New Cambridge shape.*

 Yellow Summer Glory on a demure Richmond shaped cup & saucer, with a soft, pale blue handle and foot. The rim has a touch of gold for that understated sense of elegance! Richmond shaped pieces are fairly rare to unearth and the large 8" plate alone would sell for $345.00.

🫖🫖🫖 *Footed Oleander shaped Pink Summer Glory Chintz, shown above, is quite unusual with the glossy black exterior. The gold handle and foot are easily seen against the black colour.*

🫖🫖🫖 *On the opposite page is a lovely Pink Summer Glory with a lavender exterior, also on the Footed Oleander shape. The lavender colour shows the petal details much better than the black colour above.*

Summer Glory Patterns:

#13372/S	Ripon	#13380	Cambridge
#13373/S	Henley	#13381/S	Ripon
#13374/S	Footed Oleander	#13409	Henley
#13375	Cambridge shape	#13410	Henley
#13375/S	Henley	#13417	Footed Oleander
#13376/S	Ripon	#13418	Footed Oleander
#13377/S	Ripon	#13455	
#13378	Henley	#13456	Henley
#13379	Footed Oleander		New Regent jug Pink with /53 green handle

🫖🫖🫖🫖 *Here is a Queen Anne shaped Pink Summer Glory. It is absolutely stunning! The price for such an uncommon piece would undoubtedly be quite high, $500.00 and up.*

🫖🫖🫖 *Pink Summer Glory in the classic Ripon shape is shown on the opposite page, instead of tea, a bouquet of white Hydrangeas spills out. Collectors love this pattern - it is always in vogue.*

Primrose Chintz
1 9 4 0

A favourite with collectors is the soft, delicate Primrose Chintz. It is primarily blue in colour with small clusters of yellow Primulas, or more commonly known as Primrose. The artist has done a wonderful job with this pattern. The cluster of four yellow Primula flowers are surrounded by green leaves and stems. These clusters are floating among even smaller blue Primrose blossoms. The overall character of Primrose Chintz is most feminine!

The lithographer Thomas Hulmes produced this delicate chintz.

Shelley put Primrose Chintz on: Henley, Ripon and Footed Oleander shapes. Less frequently on the Gainsborough, Boston and Queen Anne shapes. It was also applied to the Dainty shape.

I could not locate anyone with an example of Primrose Chintz on the Dainty shape. I'm sure that if a cup & saucer should be found, it would command a very high price!

🌸🌸🌸🌸🌸 *This is a very, very rare find. Primrose Chintz on the Queen Anne Shape!! A true treasure for any collector. This one was found in California.*

 Primrose Chintz is a very coveted chintz pattern. Americans seems especially eager to find the large 8" plates. Above is a Ripon cup on the left and a Footed Oleander on the right.

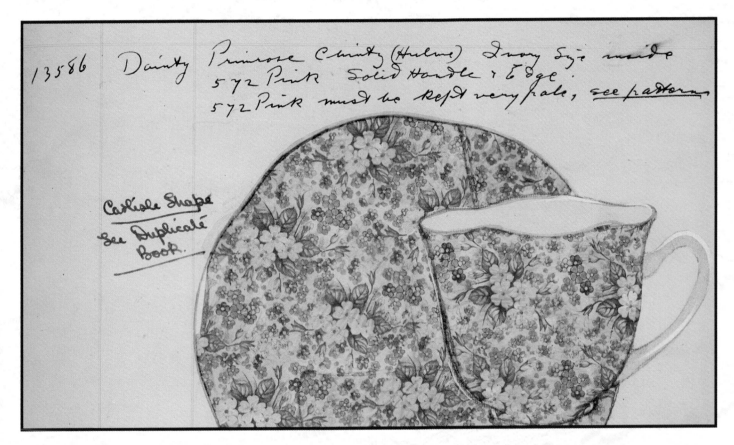

13586 Dainty Primrose Chintz (Hulme) Ivory Size inside
572 Pink Solid Handle & Edge.
572 Pink must be Kept very pale, see pattern

Carlisle Shape
See Duplicate Book.

🫖🫖🫖 *Primrose Chintz (left) on Henley shaped teapot with cups & saucers, always a favourite.*

🫖🫖🫖🫖🫖 *A Dainty shaped cup & saucer in Primrose Chintz (pattern book above) would be worth a fortune.*

🫖🫖🫖 *A reverse combination (right) with cobalt blue exterior and the chintz litho inside.*

Marguerite Chintz
1 9 4 0

Marguerite Chintz has been called the Vin Ordinaire of the chintz world. It is not a bold saucy chintz pattern but is instead most timid and quiet. Marguerite Chintz is composed of a bluish green background colour with bouquets of tiny white Marguerite daisies. A tiny bit of dark blue has been added behind the white petals of the Marguerite daisy to provide contrast and make the flower stand out. Marguerite is a very soft and delicate chintz.

Marguerite was put on the following shapes: Henley, Cambridge, Richmond, Low Oleander, Footed Oleander, Ripon and Boston!

This is not one of the more popular chintz patterns with collectors today. Given the limited number of entries found in the Shelley pattern books, I would guess that Marguerite was not extremely popular in the 1940's either.

Marguerite Chintz patterns:

#0706	Henley
#0707	Henley
#13688	Cambridge and Richmond shape
#13693	Low Oleander
#13694	Ripon
#13696	Henley
#14217	Boston
#14265	Ripon

 *Marguerite
teapot on a Henley shape.*

🫖🫖🫖🫖 *On the Queen Anne shape is Marguerite Chintz. This one comes to us from the land Down Under - Australia! Interestingly, the Queen Anne was originally called the 'Antique' shape when it was first introduced. I guess Shelley realized that such a innovative, contemporary design at the time was hardly compatible with the name 'Antique'.*

🫖 *A traditional shape, Henley with Marguerite makes a delightful teacup.*

During the 40's - 1950 Doreen Bevington (nee Oakden) worked in the offices of Shelley China. She was just a teenage girl, but had responsibility for dealing with overseas correspondence and shipping invoices. She said she would also escort customers through the Shelley showroom, until the boss arrived! Doreen had this photograph of her associates from the front office. Shown in the back row, left to right we see: Sylvia Wardle, Nora Wakelin and Millicent Bentley. On the front row, left to right, Doreen Oakden wearing a chintz dress, Jackie Gold, Eileen Corcoran and Margaret? Unfortunately we do not know Margaret's surname.

Countryside Chintz
1 9 4 0

Countryside Chintz is one of the most sought after chintz patterns today. Collectors cannot get enough of it. It is a beautiful pattern full of typical wildflowers of the English countryside. One can easily distinguish the flower of a large red Clover, Asters, yellow buttercups, pink Oxalis, blue Campanula (Harebell), pink Raspberries, blue Scabiosa (pin cushion flower) and Viola tricolour (johnny jump up, heartsease, wild pansy). The artist has done a fantastic job realistically capturing these common flowers.

Anyone wandering about the English Countryside could easily collect a bouquet of these blossoms.

The design for Countryside Chintz was produced by the artists at ceramic litho manufacturer James Davies. It utilized more colours than most chintz designs, a total of fifteen, that would have taken James Davies fifteen days to make this litho pattern.

According to the pattern books, Shelley only applied Countryside to three different shapes: Henley, Ripon and Footed Oleander. 🐝

 A Queen Anne Countryside Chintz cup - rare, rare, rare! This one resides in Alaska of all places.

🫖🫖🫖🫖 *To find Countryside Chintz on a coffee pot is quite a feat. They have been spotted in Australia and in the UK. The Henley shaped cups are easier to unearth.*

Patterns for Countryside Chintz:

| #13690 | Henley | #13701 | Ripon |
| #13700 | Footed Oleander | #13744 | Henley |

🫖🫖🫖 *Above is a delicate Footed Oleander with pink exterior. The Henley and Footed Oleander are the shapes collectors encounter most.*

🫖🫖🫖🫖🫖 *A Countryside Teapot! For years collectors speculated as to the existence of such a beast, and here we have it. This is the only example of Countryside Chintz, that I know of, on a teapot.*

A Gainsborough shaped Countryside Chintz cup and saucer with a rarely seen soft grey accent colour! This is an unusual find. Although this shape and colour combination is not mentioned in the pattern books, we are quite lucky to have this example.

Ripon Countryside cups & saucers. Expect to pay $275.00 or more for one of these!

Harmony Chintz
1956 - 1960

Harmony was never entered into the Shelley pattern books. It is an un-numbered pattern, as well as an uncontrolled chintz design. Needless to say, despite being uncontrolled it is extremely rare. Collectors almost never find this chintz.

Harmony is a very small scale patterned chintz featuring small bouquets of yellow and orange Roses and blue blossoms. It has quite a bit of white background showing through the floral bouquets. An unusual chintz because it uses the colour orange!

According to leading chintz expert Andrew Mattijssen, the Harmony lithograph was printed in Nuremberg German by the litho maker Georg Nitzke. Andrew found examples of Harmony first being used in 1938 by Dutch company Societe Ceramique in their archive books. Many other potteries, such as James Kent, A.G.Richardson, and Hollinshead & Kirkham all used the Harmony Chintz litho. When found on ware from Czechoslovakia the name Harmony is changed to Chelsea. This pattern turns up most often in Dutch chintz.

English collector John Barter says that he has seen this pattern on a Stirling shaped Bread & Butter plate. And since we know that in 1956 Eric Slater designed the Stirling shape, we can assume that Harmony was put into production from 1956 onward. Mr. Barter feels confident that a complete teaset would have been made, not just a single Bread & Butter plate. 🍵

🍵🍵🍵 *A very scarce pattern for collectors to find. It has been found in the United States, but no sightings of it in Canada, Australia, New Zealand or South Africa. Only one plate was ever found in the UK !*

* Although not found in the pattern books it has the Shelley backstamp marked on the bottom.

A Shelley Pottery factory outing, in 1952, at Rhyl, England. Shown from left to right; Alan Shelley the Sales Director, next to him is Rosamond Turner who worked as secretary to both Alan & Donald Shelley. Margaret Critchlow a shorthand typist, Barbara Smith who handled wages, Rita Mitchell, a typist & filing clerk and finally the other brother, Donald Shelley who was Technical Director.

Paisley Chintz
1 9 6 0

On June the 27th Paisley Chintz pattern #14038, was entered into the Shelley books. Some may ask - is it a chintz? We know that chintz has its beginnings in the textile world. It is first and foremost a fabric design. There is also a type of fabric design called Paisley, or boteh, which was first applied to textiles made in Kashmir India. A Paisley is a tear drop shaped design element, some say it looks more like a leaf or almond. The word Paisley is named after the Scottish town bearing the same name, a major Jacquard-loom weaving center producing huge quantities of Paisley shawls to meed demands in the 1850's. A fabric person would tell you that a Paisley is not a chintz.

Look closely at the Shelley Blue Paisley Chintz. There is more to it than just tear drop designs. There are many flowers too! Paisley Chintz has wild, fanciful stylized flowers everywhere. A huge pink venus fly-trap type flower seems to be eating another flower. Inside the Paisley itself we find a flower vase with white blossoms. The vase is sitting on blue petals. Most of the flowers are too abstract to identify, clearly showing the influence of the 'mod' style of the swinging '60's.

Paisley was made by ceramic lithograph manufacturer Thomas Hulmes. It was an uncontrolled pattern. According to author Susan Scott, Paisley was used by Wade in the 1920's and Grimwades in 1923 in green and rust colours.

In September of 1964, Paisley in a green colourway was entered into the Shelley pattern books. Shelley only put Paisley on a few different shapes: Henley, Ripon, Footed Oleander and Boston. 🐛

Paisley patterns:

#14038	Ripon	(blue)
#14042	Footed Oleander	(blue)
#14073	Henley	(blue)
#14214	Boston	(blue)
#14271	Ripon	(blue)
#14272	Ripon	(green colourway)

🐛 *A classic Henley shaped cup with Paisley Chintz.*

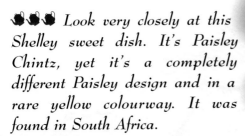 A group of Paisley Chintz Ripon cups, one done in the traditional gold trim and the other with white handle & foot! The Paisley Chintz Mini cup is very, very rare!

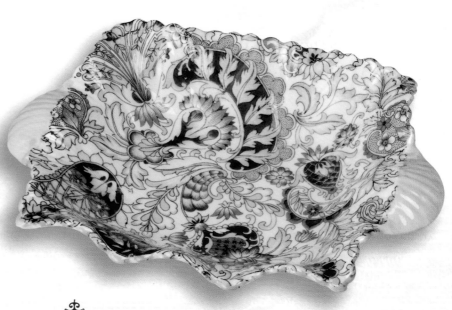 Look very closely at this Shelley sweet dish. It's Paisley Chintz, yet it's a completely different Paisley design and in a rare yellow colourway. It was found in South Africa.

Briar Rose Chintz
1 9 6 0

Here is another uncontrolled litho that was designed by Thomas Hulmes. Briar Rose is a very popular chintz with collectors. It was originally called "Lowestoft Chintz" when first entered in the pattern books in 1960. Lowestoflt is a town in England, presumably where Thomas Hulmes had his litho company. By January 12th of 1961, Shelley officially named it Briar Rose Chintz.

The word 'Briar Rose' is old English from the 16th century for hedge. A hedge would have been composed of thorny materials, like common wild blackberry and wild Rose. This chintz lithograph is delicate, cozy and very romantic. Pink and red Roses in various stages of blooming punctuate the design. Hints of purple in smaller flowers as well as green leaves and stems complete this chintz. A fair amount of white background colour shows through the flowers.

Other potteries who used Briar Rose were James Kent, Rosina China, Royal Winton, Royal Tuscan and Radfords. 🌸

Briar Rose patterns:

#2007	*Bute and New York shape*
#14039	*Ripon*
#14043	*Footed Oleander*
#14072	*Henley*
#14209	*Boston*
#14263	*Ripon*
#981	*Dainty shape*

🫖🫖🫖 *Briar Rose Chintz is much easier to find applied to the Henley shape than any other. The interior has a soft, pale pink colour that is the perfect compliment to the pinks in the chintz pattern.*

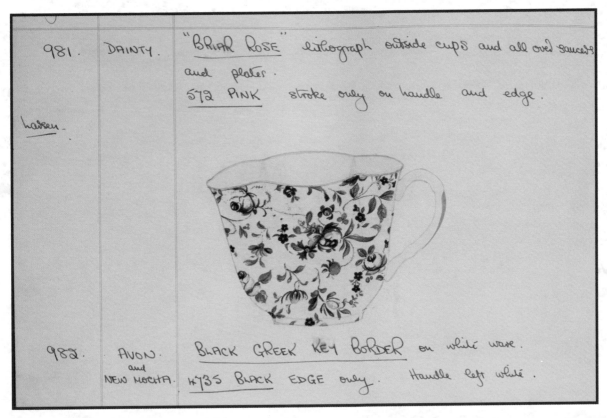

981.   DAINTY.   "BRIAR ROSE" lithograph outside cups and all over saucers and plates.
572 PINK   stroke only on handle and edge.

harken.

982.   AVON. and NEW MOCHA.   BLACK GREEK KEY BORDER on white ware.
4735 BLACK EDGE only.   Handle left white.

🫖🫖🫖🫖🫖 *The pattern book above shows the much sought after Briar Rose Chintz applied to a Dainty shaped cup! Collectors absolutely love Briar Rose and the Dainty shape is one of the most popular Shelley ever produced - making this one of the most desirable chintz pieces to have. It's unfortunate that no one has ever seen a real-life example of this cup, but collectors will keep searching.*

In the Shelley-Walker retail catalogue of January 1964 - a dozen Briar Rose Chintz in the Boston or Ripon shape cost a mere $72.00.

🫖🫖🫖 *Ripon shaped Briar Rose Chintz are very scare. Expect to pay $250.00 or more.*

 Four Teapots! That's quite a high rating for a Footed Oleander cup & saucer and a plate. Given how extremely difficult it is to attain this pattern, not just here in the States but the world over, this rating is justly deserved.

The Faces of Shelley

Taken from the pages of scrap books of former Shelley employee, Margaret Critchlow, we have three photographs showing employee outings. The first photograph was taken in 1949 at New

Brighton, a popular beach in England. Shown from left to right; Sylvia Deaville who was a wage & invoice clerk, in the center is John Evans the Assistant Art Director and on the right is Margaret Critchlow who worked as a shorthand typist.

This next photograph was taken in 1952 at Rhyl, Wales. Standing behind the bench, left to right; Ernest Waklin the chief shipping clerk and Major McEwan who was also called "The Major" or "The Traveller" since he was a sales representative who took samples of Shelley all around the country.

Seated on the bench we find, left to right; Nora Wakelin Personnel officer, Gladys Wall the wages clerk and Millicent Bentley from the accounting department.

The last photograph is also from 1952 at Rhyl. The two Shelley brothers, Donald on the left and Alan Shelley on the right, pose for the camera while standing on the beach.

Tapestry Rose Chintz
1 9 6 1

The yellow colourway of Tapestry Rose Chintz appeared late in 1961 as pattern #14125. This is an unusual chintz in that the flowers are devoid of colour. The Roses, stems and leaves are rendered in black, white and grey. The colour comes from the bold yellow or burgundy background. Tapestry Rose was an uncontrolled pattern. It can be found on ware by Grimwades (Royal Winton) in a yellow colourway and Jackson and Gosling (Grosvenor) used in both a red & blue colorway.

It was applied to four different shapes: Henley, Ripon, Footed Oleander and Boston. 🍂

Tapestry Rose Chintz patterns:

#14125	Ripon	*(yellow colourway)*
#14126	Footed Oleander	
#14184	Henley	
#14195	Henley	
#14211	Boston	
#14270	Ripon	
#14284	Ripon	
#0644	Henley shape	
#974	Henley	

🍂 *Yellow Tapestry Rose is much easier to find than the red version. This pattern is not coveted by most collectors.*

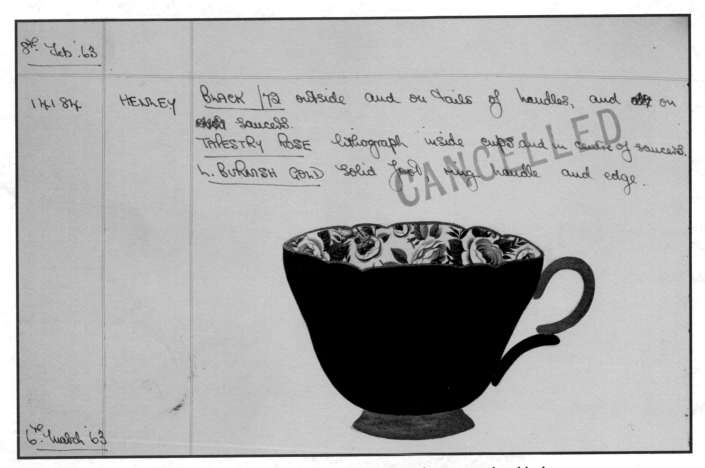

8th Feb '63

1 4 1 8 4   HENLEY   BLACK /72 outside and on tails of handles, and on saucers.
TAPESTRY ROSE lithograph inside cups and in centre of saucers.
L. BURNISH GOLD solid foot ring handle and edge.

CANCELLED

6th March '63

This is indeed unusual, a yellow Tapestry Rose inside a Henley cup with a black exterior.

🫖🫖🫖 *A Footed Oleander is uncommon, making it more expensive than the Ripon cups shown opposite.*

Black Chintz
1 9 6 3

Black Chintz is extremely scarce. It should be put on the Endangered Species List for chintz! It is the only chintz with a background colour of black, most unconventional! It is made up of yellow Daffodils, red Roses, white Daisies, blue Ipomea (morning glory) as well as a purple flower and lots of green leaves. Black Chintz is a daring, audacious chintz.

Black Chintz was designed in the studios by Dutch litho manufacturer, Mulder & Zoon (translated Miller & Son) in early 1952. It was first printed in 1957 and then again in 1960. Both times it was sold to their UK agent, K.H. Bailey. The Black Chintz litho is made up of six different colors, although it was originally intended to use eight. Making this ceramic lithograph is a lengthy process, it is only possible to print one colour per day, therefore Black Chintz would take six days to complete.

An interesting note is that actual gold is used in the metal oxides when pink and maroon colours are desired. Therefore when a pottery like Shelley would order these lithos, prices would be given depending on the cost of gold that particular day.

The selling price of these Black Chintz litho sheets in 1963, to K. H. Bailey was equal to $1.50 per sheet.

Black Chintz is an uncontrolled pattern. According the chintz collector Steven & Jennifer Phillips it was recently seen on ceramic tiles by Belgium maker Boch. Royal Standard also uses the Black Chintz litho on their range of tea ware.

Shelley only put Black Chintz on one shape - the Ripon shape. It was only entered into the pattern books one time as pattern number #14196.

Was Black Chintz ever put on a teapot? Serious collectors constantly debate this question. Many will tell you that Black Chintz was indeed put on a teapot, but that teapot disappeared, and now its memory has passed into the obscurity of legend. Others will tell you that in these enlightened days, no one believes a word of it - it is a myth.

The search continues. 🐾

If you find Black Chintz, buy it! A cup and saucer will typically sell for $575. - $650.00! Black Chintz is almost never found in Australia, Canada, New Zealand, South Africa or the United Kingdom.

Georgian Chintz
1 9 6 3

Here we have one of Decorating Manager, Ray Reynolds designs. Georgian Chintz appeared on the scene in the Seconds pattern book as #2486. Then in November of 1963 we find it again as pattern #14220. Ray decided to take the litho sheets of Georgian spray and only use one of the bouquets of flowers. He then placed this floral bouquet next to another identical one, and so on until the result was a very, very close chintz type pattern. This chintz pattern does not intertwine, the clusters of flowers are clearly separate from one another.

Georgian Chintz is composed of delightful flowers using a wide range of colours. A red Rose, white Daisy, with tiny yellow and blue blossoms scattered among the green and grey foliage completes each bouquet. The end result of Ray's creation is quite beautiful.

In a 1964 retail price list catalogue for the Shelley-Walker company of New York, Georgian Chintz has been re-named to "Oxford Rose Chintz"! Definately sounds more British! I wonder if the new name improved sales . . .?

Georgian Chintz was a success. Shelley put it on a variety of shapes: Henley, Ripon, Richmond and Boston. ❧

Georgian Chintz patterns:

#2486	*Ripon shape*
#14220	*Boston*
#14236	*Richmond*
#14273	*Ripon*
#0647	

🫖🫖🫖 *Georgian Chintz is a fairly rare pattern for collectors to find. Trios like the one shown opposite tend to be expensive, $500.00 or more for a trio is not unheard of!*

Rose Chintz
1 9 6 3

Pattern number #2487 was entered into the Shelley Seconds pattern books on October 3, 1963 under the name Rose Chintz. As the name implies, Seconds would be ware that has some tiny flaw that is found after the bisque firing. The Seconds ware pattern numbers begin with the number 2 and are only four digits long. Chintz patterns were ideal for use on Seconds since their all over multi coloured floral design would hide a multitude of sins!

Rose Chintz was another litho that Dutch company Mulder & Zoon produced. It was an uncontrolled design and can be found on Burlington Ware, Salisbury and Princess Anne English bone china. The Rose Chintz pattern is almost indistinguishable to that of Briar Rose. Collectors can easily confuse the two since the red Roses are nearly identical. Rose Chintz is a denser pattern and uses a blue flower with grey stems, where Briar Rose does not.

According to the Shelley pattern book shown below, Rose Chintz was put on the Ripon shape. I could not find anyone with an actual example of a Rose Chintz cup & saucer. My only glimpse of the rare Rose Chintz have been on square and round sweet dishes. 🌺

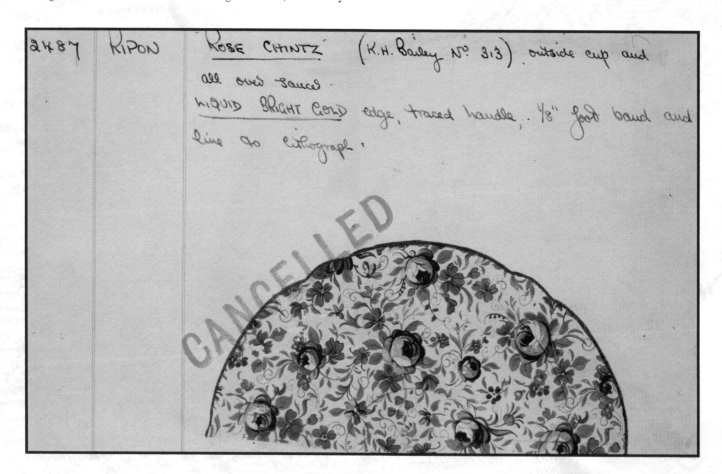

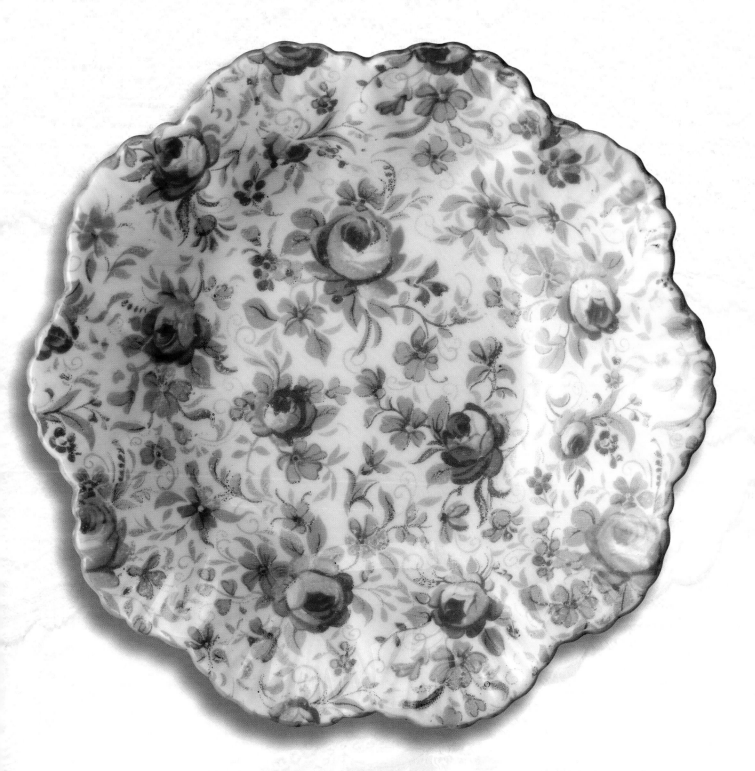

 This is another one for the Endanger Species List of Chintz. Scarce doesn't begin to describe the lack of Rose Chintz in the marketplace. Sweet dishes do not bring a very high price, however, I would speculate that a cup & saucer in this pattern would fetch an outrageous amount. And a teapot? It would go for thousands of dollars!

Rose Spray Chintz
1 9 6 3

Found in the Seconds pattern books is #2492. It is called Rose Spray Chintz and was applied to just one shape, the Ripon shape. Mr. Ray Reynolds, the Manager of Decorating at Shelley, came up with the idea for this design. He took inspiration from the popular Rose Spray pattern that had been in use since 1942. When a sheet of Rose Spray arrived from the ceramic litho maker, the sheet was covered with individual clusters of the red Roses on thorny stems. When making Rose Spray, these clusters of Roses were separated and applied in just two or three spots on the ware.

Ray thought it would be interesting to apply the entire sheet of Rose Spray to the ware, and not separate them. This would create an over all floral pattern, even though the clusters of Roses did not intertwine with one another.

I know of not a single example of Rose Spray Chintz to exist. We only have the image from the Shelley pattern book.

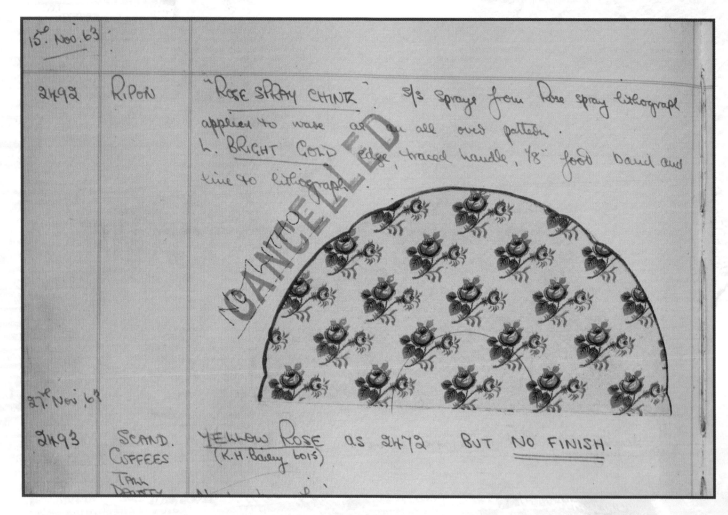

The Apprentice Program

John Rafick Soliman was one of the lucky few who entered into the Apprentice Designer program at Shelley Potteries. The Apprentice program was originally the concept of the British Pottery Manufacturers' Federation. After the war, there was a scarcity of designers working in the trade. The Federation was quite concerned about this shortage of designers for the pottery industry. They launched an aggressive campaign to entice companies to take on promising, young, talented designers.

Shelley Pottery rose to the challenge and agreed to take on several apprentice designers over a period of several years. John Soliman was one of these talented young men, working as an Apprentice Designer from 1946 until 1951. His training covered a wide range of decorating techniques; fettling, glazing, dipping, sponging, moulding, casting, throwing, and firing.

What is fettling? When pieces are cast in molds of two or more parts, they will have ridges on the ware at the seams as a result of clay build up where the mold parts join together. These ridges are called "Fettles" and the process of removing them from the clay body is called fettling. Once the piece was removed from the mold and dried, a palette knife or sponge was used to remove the seams so that no one could tell where the joins had been!

Typically, an English apprenticeship entailed part time in the potteries and part time in the school. This held true for John Soliman who spent time working with the professional designers at Shelley while attending The College of Art at Burslem in Stoke-on-Trent, two half days and several evenings each week. John recalls taking courses at the Burslem Art School in flower painting as well as traditional realistic landscape.

Bud Floral Chintz
1 9 6 4

This is one of the last chintz patterns used by Shelley Potteries. It is called something different every time it was entered into the pattern books. We know that the lithograph manufacturer, Beta Plastics, produced this pattern, and that it was their Floral Design number #826. In pattern #14274, Shelley calls this Bud Floral Chintz. The next entry calls it simply Floral Chintz. The last notation refers to it as Petite Floral Chintz.

Bud Floral is an odd looking chintz - not at all like the usual chintz designs. This is the only pattern that uses just a single flower blossom per stem. They are not connected to each other, the stems and leaves do not intertwine! The background of this chintz is a series of round oval shapes. Some collectors have said this background looks like bubbles and have coined the name "Bubble Chintz". Bud Floral isn't a true 'all over' floral design. For me, it lacks the cozy feeling I normally get with a chintz design.

No matter what name Shelley chose, it remains a curious design. One must remember that when Bud Floral was produced it was the early '60's and design trends were moving away from the warm, cozy feeling of flowers. Designers were experimenting with bold new forms, bright colours and geometric shapes.

Bud Floral was applied to three different shapes: Ripon, Boston and Henley.

We know that Bud Floral Chintz on the Henley shape was exported to Canada in April of 1965. Collectors in the United States also find the pattern.

Bud Floral Chintz patterns:

#14274	*Ripon*
#14219	*Boston*
#0604	*Henley*

🫖 *Bud Floral Chintz, shown above on the Lincoln shape, is not in huge demand by collectors. Perhaps the lack of interweaving flowers or maybe the geometric oval background - for whatever reason collectors do not seek out this chintz. This piece lives in the Great White North... Alaska.*

21st November 63

14209   BOSTON   "BRIAR ROSE" chintz inside teacups.
S9 PINK size outside cups including foot (leave white slip at
bottom of foot) S9 PINK all over saucers.
BURNISH
~~BRIGHT~~ BRIGHT GOLD edge, thick foot line, Handle solid on
top with stroke below.

E Walker

(OCT 64)
14210   BOSTON   GREEN PAISLEY
~~MELODY~~ CHINTZ inside teacups.
S3 GREEN outside including foot (leave white slip at
bottom of foot) S3 GREEN all over saucers.
BURNISH
~~BRIGHT~~ BRIGHT GOLD finish as 14209

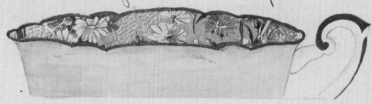

14211
14211   BOSTON   "TAPESTRY ROSE" (yellow)
S16 YELLOW SIZE
BURNISH
~~BURNISH~~ GOLD FINISH as 14209

14212   BOSTON   "BLUE DAISY"

S10 BLUE SIZE

BURNISH ~~BROST~~ GOLD FINISH as 14209

E. Walker.

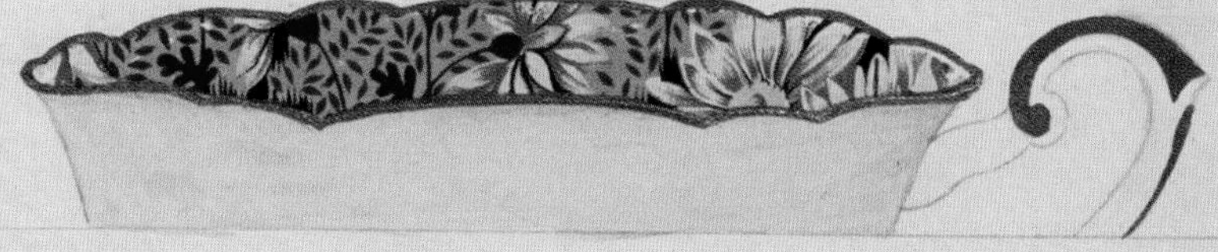

14213   BOSTON   "ROCK GARDEN"

S15 PEACH SIZE

BURNISH ~~BROST~~ GOLD FINISH as 14209

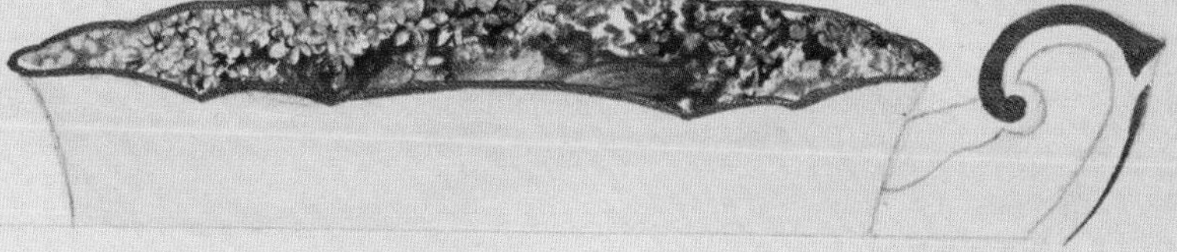

14214   BOSTON   HULME'S BLUE PAISLEY CHINTZ.

S41 MAUVE SIZE

BURNISH ~~BROST~~ GOLD FINISH as 14209

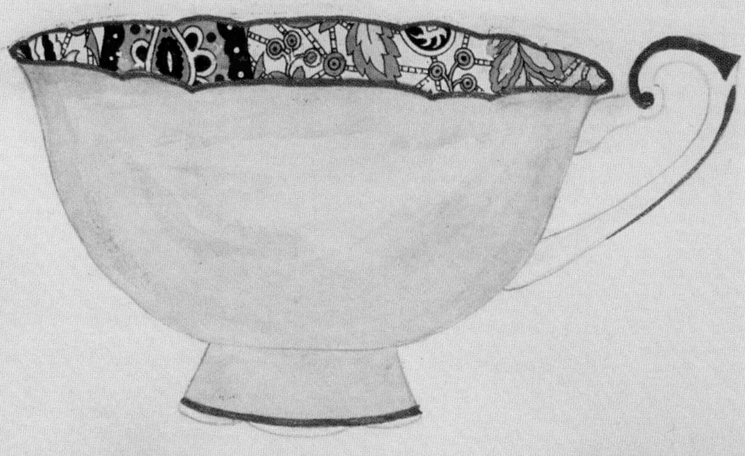

31st November '63

14215   BOSTON   "MAYTIME" Chintz inside teacups.
                   S9, PINK outside cups including foot (leave white slip at
                   bottom of foot) S9 PINK all over saucers.
E. Walker   BURNISH
                   ~~BRIGHT~~ GOLD edge. Thick foot line, Handle solid on top with
                   stroke below.

14216   BOSTON   GREEN DAISY
                   S3 GREEN SIZE
                   BURNISH
                   ~~BRIGHT~~ GOLD FINISH as 14215

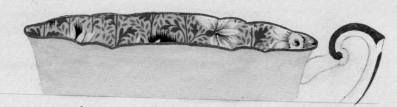

14217   BOSTON   "MARGUERITE"
                   S16 YELLOW SIZE
                   BURNISH
                   ~~BRIGHT~~ GOLD FINISH as 14215

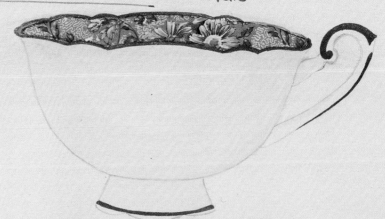

14218   BOSTON   "~~PRIMROSE~~" ~~CHINTZ~~   ^{14th April '64}   "PANSY" CHINTZ

S10 BLUE SIZE

BURNISH
~~LIGHT~~ GOLD FINISH   as 14815

E. Walker.

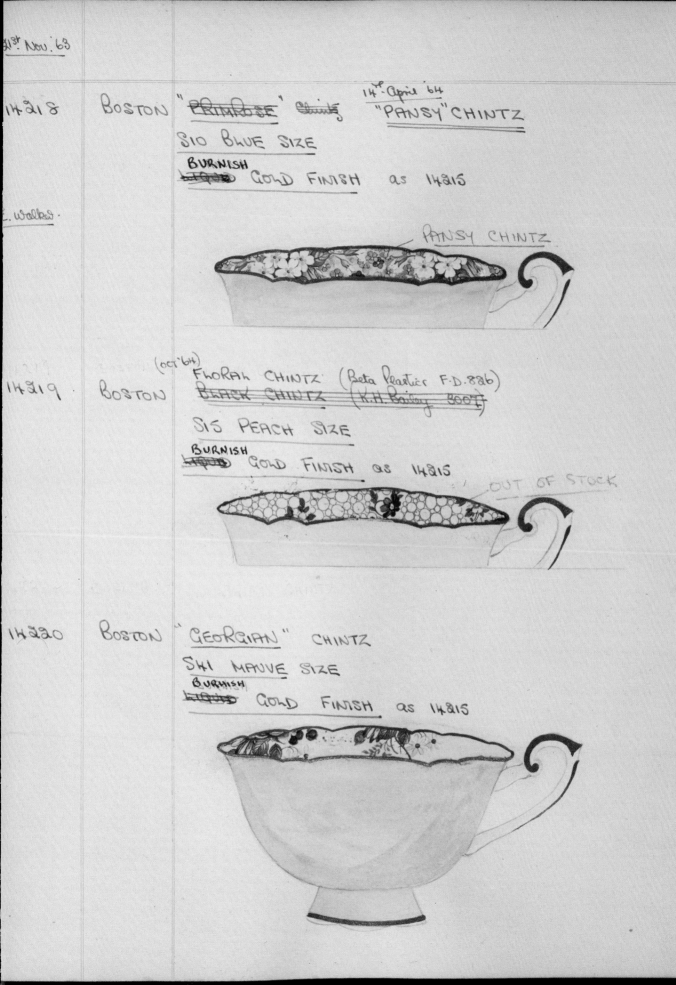

PANSY CHINTZ

14219   BOSTON   ^(oct '64) FLORAL CHINTZ (Beta Plastics F.D.826)
~~BLACK CHINTZ~~ (~~K.H.Bailey 800~~)

S15 PEACH SIZE

BURNISH
~~LIGHT~~ GOLD FINISH   as 14815

OUT OF STOCK

14220   BOSTON   "GEORGIAN" CHINTZ

S41 MAUVE SIZE

BURNISH
~~LIGHT~~ GOLD FINISH   as 14815

6½ Inches

0111   Tall   Dainty

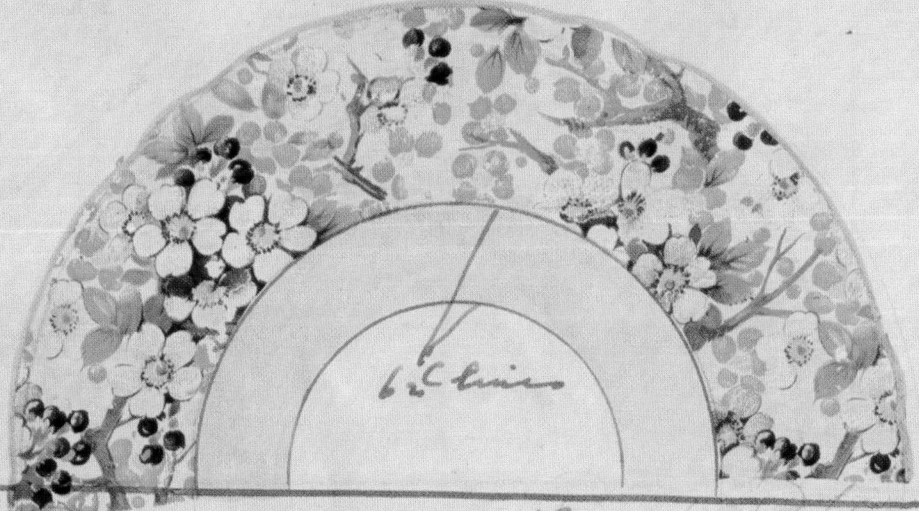

Davies Chintz litho on Ivory Size in Panels. Gilt as under with line inside cups, Traced foot line on cup

Holes
Liq. Gold

0112   low   Dainty

Ivory Size 11595 litho as under.
Gilt as under, line inside cups, foot line Traced Holes
Liq. Gold

Tpot. Handle Gilt as cup.
3 strokes on Spout. Traced
Knob no foot line on Spout
Cross on Tpot
B TB Traced

0113 Princess Litho Dainis chintz Yellow & Green on Panel
on Ivory Size. Aero Ivory Size all over plain
panels Lig Gold Edge.
Apple Green Tracing as under.

0114 Dainty May time Litho on Ivory Size, Traced in apple
Aero in Green Size on Plain panels.
Edge & Handle Lig Gold

0115 Tall Dainty Bramble on Panels (1 Hair old Gold)
Lig Gold E & line inside, Traced Handles &
foot line

C.P. goes in sheet pen.

572
Turk Blue
& 99
apple

Bibliography

The following works have been the most useful in gathering the material for this book:

Beer, Alice Baldwin, *Trade Goods*, 1970

Brickell, Christopher, *The Royal Horticultural Society Gardeners' Encyclopedia of Plants & Flowers*, London, Dorling Kindersley, 1989

Burnard, Joyce, *Chintz and Cotton*, Kangaroo Press Pty. Ltd., 1994

CARTER'S Price guide to Antiques in Australasia 1998 Edition, Sydney, Carters Publications, 1998

Davenport, Chris, *Shelley Pottery The Later Years*, Heather Publications Ltd., 1997

Eberle, Linda and Susan Scott, *The Charlton Standard Catalogue of Chintz, Second Edition*, Toronto, Charlton Press, 1997

Edward Walker Company, Sales Catalouge, 1964

Harvey, William, Robert Senft and Chris Watkins, *Shelley Potteries the History and production of a Staffordshire Family of Potters*, London, Barrie & Jenkins, 1980

Hunter, George Leland, *Decorative Textiles*, The Dean - Hick Company, 1918

Irwin, John and Brett, Katherine, *Origins of Chintz*, HMSO, 1970

NSCC Newsletter, Volume 8, Issue 3, Fall 1997, *Shelley Chintz Treasures*, Curt & Lynne Leiser.

Shelley Group Publication, *Chuck Out Your Chintz!*, John Barter, UK 1999

The original Shelley Pottery Pattern Books, Royal Doulton Limited, UK

The archives and sales records of Mulder & Zoon, Amsterdam, The Netherlands

The archives and sales records at Capper-Ratauds, UK

The archives of Thomas Hulmes, Capper-Ratauds, UK

The archives of James Davies, Johnson Matthey, UK

Acknowledgements

The author would like to thank Royal Doulton plc for their kind permission to reproduce extracts from the Shelley pattern books. Products listed or shown were manufactured by Shelley China Ltd, now a subsidiary of Royal Doulton. This book has been produced and published independently. The author/publisher has no connection with Royal Doulton, and any opinions expressed in the book are strictly those of the author alone and not endorsed by Royal Doulton.

In regards to this book's actual creation, I am indebted to Shelley collectors from Australia, Canada, England and the United States who allowed me the honour of photographing their treasured chintz. Without their help and support this book would never have happened! A special thanks to:

John Barter, Dianne Brackett, Graham & Sue Bourne, John Comstock, Cheryl Daysh, Anji Davis, Joel Davidson, Jan Dodson, Linda Ellis, Rochelle Hart, Gary Hoare, Shelley Santora-Jones, Pat Kazarian, Carolyn Keating, Curt & Lynn Leiser, Grant & Karen Loemker, Gene & Marsha Loveland, Sally Moore, Mary Ann Null, Judy & Howard Osborne, Pearl Jacks Ross, Dianne Smith, Lyn Smith, Mark & Shelley Sweeney, Lora Thurber, Susan Willis, Bob Woods.

Mr. Ray Reynolds for his endless source of knowledge on the workings at Shelley Pottery. A special thanks to his wife Elsie for all those 'jammy dodgers' & cups of tea!

Chris Davenport, he kept me going especially when I ran into obstacles. He has been most generous with information on the entire book writing process, letting me learn from his past experience.

I owe a huge debt of thanks to Andrew Mattijssen for all his help. He was invaluable to me when researching Mulder & Zoon in the Netherlands, as well as info on 'uncontrolled' chintz patterns. He is one of the most knowledgeable chintz collectors!

Julie McKeown, Joan Jones and Sandra Baddiley of Royal Doulton for putting up with me for an entire week while I poked & prodded through the Shelley Pattern Books.

Julie Carter, Editor of Carters Magazine in Sydney, Australia who coordinated the photography of those Shelley items Down Under!

Val Shelley and the Gladstone Museum, Stoke-on-Trent, England. Everyone from the U.K. Shelley Group and the National Shelley China Club, U.S.A.

I was touched to receive so many B & W photos of loved ones who worked for Shelley Pottery. Space limitations prevented me from using them all, however I would like to thank everyone who helped: Chris Aves, Doreen Bevington, Gail Brown, Doris (Dee) Johnson Fawcett, Katherine Kavanagh, Ray & Elsie Reynolds, Denis Roberts, John Soliman, Douglas Wakefield.

Finally to my family and friends: Sue Brown, Paul & Victoria Hutton, Pat Kazarian, Beth Moran & Steve Wade! Also Cliff & Lyn Chiet, Ginny Moran, Kelly & Larry Pezor, Ron Wade and Liam Wade. Thanks guys I'd be lost without you!

And of course I would be remiss if I forgot to thank Dave my designer who at the beginning of this project didn't know his bum from a Henley or a Ripon... I raise a Blue Sapphire Martini in his honor.

Final Notes

Shelley is a widely collected treasure, and over the past few years clubs have formed of these individuals. They are wonderful places to gain information, meet fellow collectors as well as seeing examples of Shelley bone china. These clubs have "get togethers" several times a year and distribute a newsletter.

National Shelley China Club
National Shelley China Club is based in the United States. For a copy of the newsletter please contact the editor, Mr. Curt Leiser at 12010 38th Avenue, Seattle Washington 98125. He can also be reached via E-Mail at: cleiser@compuserve.com. Club subscriptions are renewable each year on April 1 for $35.00 ($40.00 for non US residence). The newsletter is produced four times a year, while once a year this club holds a huge convention in different cities all over the country.

The Shelley Group
U.K. Shelley Club also has a newsletter coming out four times per year. Membership to this group for an individual membership is 25.00 GBP or $42.00. A family membership rate is 30.00 GBP or $50.00 per year. The club Treasurer, Linda Ellis can be reached at 228 Croyland Road, Lower Edmonton, London N9 7BG ENGLAND. For Americans unable to pay for a club membership in Sterling, an alternative method of paying in US dollars is available by contacting Mr. Mannie Banner at: 6412 Silverbrooke West, West Bloomfield, Michigan 48322.

Australian Shelley Club
Australian Shelley Club - was established in 1983 making it the oldest of the three collector clubs. They have a newsletter four times per year. Membership is AUS $20.00 whether for an individual or family. Mr. Greg Hammond should be contacted for membership information at: greghmnd@nrg.com.au

New Zealand Shelley Collectors Group
New Zealand Shelley Collectors Group is a small club that meet about four times per year at individual members homes. June Hearne is the editor of the newsletter and can be reached at: june.hearne@adis.co.nz or by writing to The Shelley Collectors Club, Glenys Ryall, 9 Fowey Avenue, Te Atatu South, Auckland.

For individuals with access to a computer and the internet, there is a delightful on-line forum called The Shelley List. There are over 250+ enthusiastic Shelley collectors on line to discuss prices, great shops for Shelley, shapes, unusual patterns, etc. Membership is free, simply send an E-Mail to: majordomo@capaccess.org then in the body of your email type only this line: subscribe shelleychina.

A similar on-line community of collectors exists for chintz! It is aptly called the ChintzNet and is the brainchild of Jennifer and Steven Phillips. Their site has many quality dealers of Shelley chintz as well as chintz produced by other potteries! The web page is located at: http://www.chintznet.com/

Additional Reading:
A superior source for information on Shelley is Chris Davenport's book *Shelley Pottery - The Later Years* by Heather Publishing. The ISBN number is: 0 9530242 0 2. This UK publishers telephone/fax number is: 011 44 1260 279618.

Susan Scott's book on chintz including a valuable price guide is called *The Charlton Standard Catalogue of Chintz - Third Edition*. It shows all the chintz patterns produced by all the major Potteries. To get a signed copy by the author, please see the ChintzNet web site for details.